God's
CHARACTER

THE BEST NEWS IN THE UNIVERSE!

Camp Meeting 2001
by Dr. Elliot Douglin

God's
CHARACTER
THE BEST NEWS IN THE UNIVERSE!

Camp Meeting 2001
By Dr. Elliot Douglin

Truth for the Final Generation
P.O. Box 725
Bridgetown, Barbados, W.I.
Tel/Fax (246) 421-7790
email: tffgbgi@yahoo.com
      info@tffgbarbados.com

Visit us on the web at **www.truthforthefinalgeneration1984.org**
or **www.tffgbarbados.com**

Printed in Barbados

Cover design and book design by Sawtooth Graphics, Caldwell, ID, USA

Preface

This book, *"God's Character: The Best News in the Universe!"* is a study of the character of God from the *Bible and Bible alone,* allowing scripture to interpret scripture. It is dedicated to the on-going search for truth and the advancing light, which results from such scriptural research.

But this book goes even further and analyses the revelation of God's Agapé love as it is demonstrated in the gift of His Son for the redemption of mankind and for the clarification of the issues involved in the great cosmic conflict between light and darkness.

> *"Let us try to know the Lord. He will come to us as surely as the day dawns, as surely as the spring rains fall upon the earth."* Hosea 6:3 (TEV).

Knowing and experiencing the knowledge of God as revealed in the life, death and resurrection of Jesus Christ, will give victory over lukewarmness and will produce a love-motivated, heart-felt, surrender which will be absolute and which will usher in the final showers of the Latter Rain of the Holy Spirit!

Contents

Contents

Introduction

"But we all, with open face beholding as in a glass the glory of the Lord, are changed into the same image from glory to glory." 2 Cor. 3:18.

By dwelling upon the love of God and His Son, by contemplating the perfection of the divine character and claiming the righteousness of Christ as ours by faith, we are transformed into the same image!

It is through the last generation of true believers that God will fully reflect His character to the world. How important, then, for us, in these last days of earth's history to correctly understand and fully experience the love and character of God.

God's end-time people must receive the "Latter Rain" of the Holy Spirit in order to finish God's work in the earth. This "Latter Rain" includes both an intellectual and an experiential knowledge of God's character—His perfect love, wisdom and righteousness as revealed through Jesus Christ.

We have come to the time when every belief, regardless of how popular or how long-standing it may be, must be thoroughly tested by the word of God by allowing scripture to interpret itself. In these last days Bible truth is exposing religious error.

In this book, the traditional view of a God who destroys His enemies by violent, cruel, coercive measures is scrutinized and subjected to careful scriptural analysis. The reader is invited to examine all the evidences honestly, objectively and carefully and see where the weight of evidence leads.

We must know the truth about this matter because our character transformation can rise no higher than our conception of God's character. If we have a faulty picture of the divine character our own characters will in turn be faulty.

Bible prophecy predicts an unprecedented revelation of the true knowledge of God's character in the end-time. Here are a few examples.

"Then shall we know if we follow on to know the Lord: His going forth is prepared as the morning; and He shall come unto us as the rain, as the latter and former rain unto the earth." Hosea 6:3.

"For the earth shall be filled with the knowledge of the glory of the Lord as the waters cover the sea." Habakkuk 2:14.

"Arise, shine; for thy light is come, and the glory of the Lord is risen upon thee. For behold, the darkness shall cover the earth and gross darkness the people: but the Lord shall arise upon thee. And the gentiles shall come to thy light, and kings to the brightness of thy rising." Isaiah 60:1-3.

The reader is invited to look to Christ, to behold the attractive loveliness of His character, and by beholding, become changed into His likeness. The mist that intervenes between Christ and the soul will be rolled back as you look by faith past the hellish shadow of Satanic tradition and see God's glorious character revealed in the righteousness of Christ.

Satan's constant work is to hide Jesus from our sight, to darken His light by tradition and misinterpretation; but when we get a glimpse of His glory, we will be attracted to Him. Sin hides the beautiful character of Christ from our view. Prejudice, popular religious tradition, false views of our Heavenly Father, self-righteousness and passion blind our eyes so that we do not discern the Saviour. Oh, if we would draw near to God by faith, He would reveal to us His glory, which is His character. And by knowing Him aright we would love, admire, adore and willingly obey Him because of His great love for us, manifested in the gift of His Son.

Indeed to know God aright is to love Him.

In spite of all the opposition to the knowledge of the *true* character of God message and the *true* gospel of Jesus Christ, the truth will triumph and the *"remnant"* will triumph with it.

May the Holy Spirit guide you into all truth as you read. Remember that God has promised that in these latter days light on "His anger, His wrath and how He punishes," will be perfectly understood by His people!

"The anger of the Lord shall not return, until he have executed, and till he have performed the thoughts of his heart: in the latter days ye shall consider it perfectly." Jeremiah 23:20.

"The Lord's anger is a storm, a furious wind that will rage over the heads of the wicked. It will not end until he has done all that he intends to do, in days to come his people will understand this clearly." Jeremiah 30: 23,24 (TEV).

One

The Importance Of The Knowledge Of God

"And this is life eternal, that they might know thee the only true God, and Jesus Christ, whom thou hast sent." John 17:3

This profound declaration comes straight from the mouth of Jesus Himself. Our Saviour is not one to waste words. The knowledge of the only true God and His Son is indeed eternal life! Without this knowledge, the professed people of God would (eventually) be overcome by Satan.

"My people are destroyed for lack of knowledge: because thou hast rejected knowledge, I will also reject thee, that thou shalt be no priest to me: seeing thou hast forgotten the law of thy God, I will also forget thy children." Hosea 4:6.

In fact, God invites us, implores and even admonishes us to **know** and **understand** Him.

"Thus saith the Lord, Let not the wise man glory in his wisdom, neither let the mighty man glory in his might, let not the rich man glory in his riches: But let him that glorieth glory in this, that he understandeth and knoweth me, that I am the Lord which exercise lovingkindness, judgment, and righteousness, in the earth: for in these things I delight, saith the Lord." Jer. 9:23, 24.

What a wonderful text of scripture! God wants us to **know** and **to understand** Him; especially in His work of exercising loving kindness (mercy), judgment and righteousness (justice) in the earth. Without this knowledge of God there can be no real victory over sin!

> *"Awake to righteousness, and sin not; for some have not the knowledge of God: I speak this to your shame." 1 Cor. 15:34.*

Moreover, the experience of "following on to know the Lord" (YAHWEH) is in fact declared to be the experience of the latter-rain of the Holy Spirit!

> *"Then shall we know, if we follow on to know the Lord: his going forth is prepared as the morning; and he shall come unto us as the rain, as the latter and former rain unto the earth." Hosea 6:3*

The Apostle Paul became very excited about the importance of the knowledge of God. He was almost beside himself as he wrote these words recorded in Eph. 3:17-21.

> *"That Christ may dwell in your hearts by faith; that ye, being rooted and grounded in love, May be able to comprehend with all saints what is the breadth, and length, and depth, and height; And to know the love of Christ, which passeth knowledge, that ye might be filled with all the fulness of God. Now unto him that is able to do exceeding abundantly above all that we ask or think, according to the power that worketh in us, Unto him be glory in the church by Christ Jesus throughout all ages, world without end. Amen." Eph. 3:17-21.*

Look again at verse 19:

> *"And to know the love of Christ, which passeth knowledge, that ye might be filled with all the fulness of God."*

The love of God is beyond knowledge and yet we are challenged to **know** it! This is the highest and greatest education and development open to human beings.

Are you, dear reader, ready to acquire this knowledge? And, more importantly, are you ready to experience it?

Two

The Formula For Learning The Knowledge Of God

To know and understand the truth, we must learn to compare scripture with scripture and in so doing let scripture interpret scripture. In other words, we must compare spiritual things with spiritual, as Paul tells us in 1 Cor. 2:13:

> *"Which things also we speak, not in the words which man's wisdom teacheth, but which the Holy Ghost teacheth; comparing spiritual things with spiritual." 1 Cor. 2:13.*

Prayerful, careful, thorough, exhaustive study is required for the correct interpretation of the scriptures.

> *"And that from a child thou hast known the holy scriptures, which are able to make thee wise unto salvation through faith which is in Christ Jesus. All scripture is given by inspiration of God, and is profitable for doctrine, for reproof, for correction, for instruction in righteousness: That the man of God may be perfect, thoroughly furnished unto all good works." 2 Tim. 3:15-17.*

> *"Study to shew thyself approved unto God, a workman that needeth not to be ashamed, rightly dividing the word of truth." 2 Tim. 2:15.*

"Rightly dividing the word of truth" requires the application of Isaiah's method of study.

> *"For precept must be upon precept, precept upon precept; line upon line, line upon line; here a little, and there a little." Isaiah 28:10.*

The Holy Spirit, in and through the word of God, will teach the honest, sincere searcher and guide him or her into all truth.

> *"Howbeit when he, the Spirit of truth, is come, he will guide you into all truth: for he shall not speak of himself; but whatsoever he shall hear, that shall he speak: and he will shew you things to come." John 16:13*

> *"For the word of God is quick, and powerful, and sharper than any two-edged sword, piercing even to the dividing asunder of soul and spirit, and of the joints and marrow, and is a discerner of the thoughts and intents of the heart." Hebrews 4:12*

> *"It is the spirit that quickeneth; the flesh profiteth nothing: the words that I speak unto you, they are spirit, and they are life." John 6:63*

> *"Search the scriptures; for in them ye think ye have eternal life: and they are they which testify of me." John 5:39.*

Moreover, a willingness to do the will of God is necessary to understand true doctrine.

> *"If any man will do his will, he shall know of the doctrine, whether it be of God, or whether I speak of myself." John 7:17.*

> *"And ye shall know the truth, and the truth shall make you free." John 8:32*

> *"For we can do nothing against the truth, but for the truth." 2 Cor. 13:8*

Remember too that the knowledge of truth is progressive.

> *"But the path of the just is as the shining light, that shineth more and more unto the perfect day." Proverbs 4:18*

> *"But as it is written, Eye hath not seen, nor ear heard, neither have entered into the heart of man, the things which God hath prepared for them that love him. But God hath revealed them unto us by his Spirit: for the Spirit searcheth all things, yea, the deep things of God. For what man knoweth the things of a man, save the spirit of man which is in him? even so the things of God knoweth no man, but the Spirit of God. Now we have received, not the spirit of the world, but the spirit which is of God; that we might know the things that are freely given to us of God. Which things also we speak, not in the words which man's wisdom teacheth, but which the Holy Ghost teacheth; comparing spiritual things with spiritual.*

But the natural man receiveth not the things of the Spirit of God: for they are foolishness unto him: neither can he know them, because they are spiritually discerned. But he that is spiritual judgeth all things, yet he himself is judged of no man. For who hath known the mind of the Lord, that he may instruct him? But we have the mind of Christ." 1 Cor. 2:9-16.

"But if we walk in the light, as he is in the light, we have fellowship one with another, and the blood of Jesus Christ his Son cleanseth us from all sin." 1 John 1:7

Progressive cleansing from sin requires the progressive impartation of truth and walking in the light! And Jesus is the Light of the world!

Three

The Knowledge Of God Revealed Through Jesus Christ

In the plan of redemption, the knowledge of God is supremely and most clearly revealed in and through Jesus Christ. Indeed, to "see" Jesus is to "see" the Father.

> *"Jesus saith unto him, Have I been so long time with you, and yet hast thou not known me, Philip? he that hath seen me hath seen the Father; and how sayest thou then, Shew us the Father?" John 14:9*

Through the incarnation, earthly life, sacrificial death and resurrection of the Son of God, the knowledge of the character of God has been most clearly revealed to the universe.

> *"In the beginning was the Word, and the Word was with God, and the Word was God. The same was in the beginning with God. All things were made by him; and without him was not any thing made that was made. In him was life; and the life was the light of men. And the light shineth in darkness; and the darkness comprehended it not... And the Word was made flesh, and dwelt among us, (and we beheld his glory, the glory as of the only begotten of the Father,) full of grace and truth. For the law was given by Moses, but grace and truth came by Jesus Christ. No man hath seen God at any time; the only begotten Son, which is in the bosom of the Father, he hath declared him." John 1:1-5, 14, 17, 18.*

It should be very clear then that every statement about God in the Bible must be understood in the light of the knowledge of God as revealed through Jesus Christ. Indeed the light of the knowledge of the glory, the character, of God shines in the face of Jesus Christ.

> *"For God, who commanded the light to shine out of darkness, hath shined in our hearts, to give the light of the knowledge of the glory of God in the face of Jesus Christ." 2 Cor. 4:6.*

Jesus Christ is God's ultimate and clearest statement or message about Himself. This means that all previous statements about God must be, and can only be, correctly interpreted and fully understood by the life, death and resurrection of our Lord Jesus Christ.

> *"For the law was given by Moses, but grace and truth came by Jesus Christ. No man hath seen God at any time; the only begotten Son, which is in the bosom of the Father, he hath declared him." John 1:17, 18*

> *"God, who at sundry times and in divers manners spake in time past unto the fathers by the prophets, Hath in these last days spoken unto us by his Son, whom he hath appointed heir of all things, by whom also he made the worlds; Who being the brightness of his glory, and the express image of his person, and upholding all things by the word of his power, when he had by himself purged our sins, sat down on the right hand of the Majesty on high;" Hebrews 1:1-3*

And what message did Jesus give about His Father? John gives the answer in 1 John 1:5.

> *"This then is the message which we have heard of him, and declare unto you, that God is light, and in him is no darkness at all." 1 John 1:5.*

Therefore God cannot be, can never be the source of darkness. Darkness means sin and its results. Light means truth and righteousness and the results of righteousness.

> *"And this is the condemnation, that light is come into the world, and men loved darkness rather than light, because their deeds were evil. For every one that doeth evil hateth the light, neither cometh to the light, lest his deeds should be reproved. But he that doeth truth cometh to the light, that his deeds may be made manifest, that they are wrought in God." John 3:19-21*

Since Jesus is *"the way, the truth and the life,"* no man can come to the Father or understand the Father's character except through the Son. Jesus came to earth to declare, to reveal, to testify of His Father's character. Jesus is the faithful and true witness and His message concerning the Father's character is called "the testimony of Jesus, which is the Spirit of Prophecy."

Therefore, all the true prophets have declared that *"God is light and in Him is no darkness at all."*

> *"The Revelation of Jesus Christ, which God gave unto him, to shew unto his servants things which must shortly come to pass; and he sent and signified it by his angel unto his servant John: Who bare record of the word of God, and of the testimony of Jesus Christ, and of all things that he saw... And from Jesus Christ, who is the faithful witness, and the first begotten of the dead, and the prince of the kings of the earth. Unto him that loved us, and washed us from our sins in his own blood."* Rev. 1:1,2,5.

> *"And I fell at his feet to worship him. And he said unto me, See thou do it not: I am thy fellowservant, and of thy brethren that have the testimony of Jesus: worship God: for the testimony of Jesus is the spirit of prophecy."* Rev. 19:10

> *"Of which salvation the prophets have enquired and searched diligently, who prophesied of the grace that should come unto you: Searching what, or what manner of time the Spirit of Christ which was in them did signify, when it testified beforehand the sufferings of Christ, and the glory that should follow."* 1 Peter 1:10-11

Yes friend, if you really see Jesus you see His Father!

Four

Words Can Be Misleading

Human language has its limitations.

A particular word in one language can express a particular meaning, but may not be as accurately conveyed by its equivalent translation into another language.

The Bible was originally written in very ancient languages; the Old Testament in Hebrew and the New Testament in Greek. Translators down through the centuries have done their best to be as accurate as possible in the translation of the words, phrases, sentences, and idioms of those ancient languages, yet limitations and difficulties of translation are evident.

We call this the **language problem**.

This is why we must allow scripture to interpret itself. Instead of interpreting a difficult Biblical word according to our modern meaning of that word, we must let the Bible interpret the Biblical meaning and demonstrate the Biblical linguistic usage of that particular word.

> *"Which things also we speak, not in the words which man's wisdom teacheth, but which the Holy Ghost teacheth; comparing spiritual things with spiritual." 1 Cor. 2:13.*

Let us consider the words *eternal, forever, everlasting, forever and ever*, in our English translations.

These words are used to translate the Hebrew word *OLAM* in the Old Testament or the Greek word *AIONIOS* in the New Testament. But those ancient words do not really mean what our modern words like *eternal* and *forever* mean.

This has led to an incorrect understanding of the term *eternal fire* or *everlasting fire*. Many Christians believe *"aionios"* fire (translated "eternal" fire) will never stop burning but will burn literally forever and ever!

Let us apply the fundamental rule of 1 Cor. 2:13 and, by comparing spiritual things with spiritual, find out what the Bible means by the words *eternal*, or *forever* or *everlasting* (Hebrew: *OLAM*; Greek: *AIONIOS*). Even if a student of the Bible knew nothing of the original ancient languages, he or she could still easily arrive at the true meaning and correct usage of the words.

Sodom and Gomorrah were burned by *eternal* fire.

> *"Even as Sodom and Gomorrah, and the cities about them in like manner, giving themselves over to fornication, and going after strange flesh, are set forth for an example, suffering the vengeance of eternal fire."* Jude v7

The *eternal* fire burned Sodom and Gomorrah to ashes.

> *"And turning the cities of Sodom and Gomorrah into ashes condemned them with an overthrow, making them an ensample unto those that after should live ungodly;"* 2 Peter 2:6

Furthermore the *eternal* fire consumed these cities rather quickly.

> *"For the punishment of the iniquity of the daughter of my people is greater than the punishment of the sin of Sodom, that was overthrown as in a moment, and no hands stayed on her."* Lam. 4:6

Similarly, in the end, *eternal* fire will burn up the unsaved to ashes.

> *"For, behold, the day cometh, that shall burn as an oven; and all the proud, yea, and all that do wickedly, shall be stubble: and the day that cometh shall burn them up, saith the Lord of hosts, that it shall leave them neither root nor branch. But unto you that fear my name shall the Sun of righteousness arise with healing in his wings; and ye shall go forth, and grow up as calves of the stall. And ye shall tread down the wicked; for they shall be ashes under the soles of your feet in the day that I shall do this, saith the Lord of hosts."* Mal. 4:1-3

> *"But the wicked shall perish, and the enemies of the Lord shall be as the fat of lambs: they shall consume; into smoke shall they consume away."* Psalm 37:20

In fact the wicked will be as though they had never been!

"For as ye have drunk upon my holy mountain, so shall all the heathen drink continually, yea, they shall drink, and they shall swallow down, and they shall be as though they had not been." Obadiah 16

"Let the sinners be consumed out of the earth, and let the wicked be no more. Bless thou the Lord, O my soul. Praise ye the Lord." Psalm 104:35

This final destruction of unrepentant sinners is called the second death.

"He that overcometh shall inherit all things; and I will be his God, and he shall be my son. But the fearful, and unbelieving, and the abominable, and murderers, and whoremongers, and sorcerers, and idolaters, and all liars, shall have their part in the lake which burneth with fire and brimstone: which is the second death." Rev. 21:7,8

It is indeed a fact, that whereas the gift of God is literally endless and perfect life, the wages of sin is permanent death, annihilation.

"For the wages of sin is death; but the gift of God is eternal life through Jesus Christ our Lord." Romans 6:23

We can clearly see then that the ancient words *OLAM* in the Hebrew and *AIONIOS* in the Greek, both translated *eternal* in the English, simply mean *a duration of time which lasts as long as the subject lasts.*

Jonah said he was in the bottom of the sea *forever* while it was actually "three days and three nights":

"I went down to the bottoms of the mountains; the earth with her bars was about me for ever: yet hast thou brought up my life from corruption, O Lord my God." Jonah 2:6

Therefore eternal fire lasts as long as it takes to burn its victims to ashes, and nothing can quench it until its work is done. And the converse is true, eternal life will last forever because it is the life of the eternal God, who has no end.

This truth also exposes another popular error. There is a popular religious belief, held by many Christians, that the human soul is immortal. The word *immortal* means *not subject to death, cannot die, indestructible.* The Bible teaches quite clearly that the human soul is very much mortal.

"Behold, all souls are mine; as the soul of the father, so also the soul of the son is mine: the soul that sinneth, it shall die." Ezekiel 18:4

> *"Let him know, that he which converteth the sinner from the error of his way shall save a soul from death, and shall hide a multitude of sins."* James 5:20

In fact, only God has immortality.

> *"Which in his times he shall shew, who is the blessed and only Potentate, the King of kings, and Lord of lords; Who only hath immortality, dwelling in the light which no man can approach unto; whom no man hath seen, nor can see: to whom be honour and power everlasting. Amen."* 1 Tim. 6:15,16

We are invited to seek for immortality. If we possessed it naturally we would not need to seek for it.

> *"Who will render to every man according to his deeds: To them who by patient continuance in well doing seek for glory and honour and immortality, eternal life:"* Rom. 2:6,7

Only the saved have eternal life, no unsaved person has eternal life.

> *"And this is the record, that God hath given to us eternal life, and this life is in his Son. He that hath the Son hath life; and he that hath not the Son of God hath not life."* 1 John 5:11,12.

> *"Whosoever hateth his brother is a murderer: and ye know that no murderer hath eternal life abiding in him."* 1 John 3:15.

Immortality will be given to the saved at the Second Coming of Christ.

> *"Behold, I shew you a mystery; We shall not all sleep, but we shall all be changed, In a moment, in the twinkling of an eye, at the last trump: for the trumpet shall sound, and the dead shall be raised incorruptible, and we shall be changed. For this corruptible must put on incorruption, and this mortal must put on immortality. So when this corruptible shall have put on incorruption, and this mortal shall have put on immortality, then shall be brought to pass the saying that is written, Death is swallowed up in victory."* 1 Cor. 15: 51-54.

> *"For the Lord himself shall descend from heaven with a shout, with the voice of the archangel, and with the trump of God: and the dead in Christ*

shall rise first: Then we which are alive and remain shall be caught up together with them in the clouds, to meet the Lord in the air: and so shall we ever be with the Lord." 1 Thess. 4:16,17.

"And death and hell were cast into the lake of fire. This is the second death. And whosoever was not found written in the book of life was cast into the lake of fire." Rev. 20:14,15

For those who reject God's salvation, both soul and body will be destroyed in the final fires of Gehenna at the end of the millennium as seen in Revelation 20.

"And fear not them which kill the body, but are not able to kill the soul: but rather fear him which is able to destroy both soul and body in hell." Matt. 10:28.

"For, behold, the day cometh, that shall burn as an oven; and all the proud, yea, and all that do wickedly, shall be stubble: and the day that cometh shall burn them up, saith the Lord of hosts, that it shall leave them neither root nor branch. But unto you that fear my name shall the Sun of righteousness arise with healing in his wings; and ye shall go forth, and grow up as calves of the stall. And ye shall tread down the wicked; for they shall be ashes under the soles of your feet in the day that I shall do this, saith the Lord of hosts." Mal. 4:1-3.

"For God so loved the world, that he gave his only begotten Son, that whosoever believeth in him should not perish, but have everlasting life." John. 3:16

"For the wages of sin is death; but the gift of God is eternal life through Jesus Christ our Lord." Romans 6:23

"And death and hell were cast into the lake of fire. This is the second death. And whosoever was not found written in the book of life was cast into the lake of fire." Rev. 20:14,15

Five

Introducing the Divine Nature

The world is man-centered. Even the church is far more man-centered than God-centered. Christians, generally speaking, seem to be preoccupied with knowing more about themselves and other subjects than knowing more about God. If God is not our primary focus then everything else will soon get out of focus.

The most important thing in life is knowing God better.

The man-centered focus that has crept into today's church must be resisted at all costs. Matters such as family life, child discipline, church finances should be addressed, but we must be careful that "market forces" do not mold our theology. People may want to know about these issues, but what they need primarily, is to know God.

The things of the world absorb too much of our time and attention, and the result of all this is that God has become marginalized. If we were to pay as much attention to the things that pertain to God as we do to the things that pertain to the world, then the spiritual health of the church would be far better than it is now.

Through the prophet Jeremiah, God speaks to us and shows us that His greatest desire is that we should come to know Him:

> *"Thus saith the Lord, Let not the wise man glory in his wisdom, neither let the mighty man glory in his might, let not the rich man glory in his riches: But let him that glorieth glory in this, that he understandeth and knoweth me, that I am the Lord which exercise lovingkindness, judgment, and righteousness, in the earth: for in these things I delight, saith the Lord."* Jer. 9:23, 24.

And remember the words of Jesus:

"And this is life eternal, that they might know thee the only true God, and Jesus Christ, whom thou hast sent." John 17:3.

God Is Eternal In The Absolute Sense Of The Word

The first fact we need to appreciate in the study of God is that the Godhead is absolutely eternal, that is, **without beginning** and **without end!**

"And God said unto Moses, I AM THAT I AM: and he said, Thus shalt thou say unto the children of Israel, I AM hath sent me unto you." Exodus 3:14.

The Hebrew words translated I AM THAT I AM are EHYEH ASHER EHYEH. This mysterious term indicates the **continuous present tense**: it indicates self-existence and signifies **beginninglessness and endlessness**.

When the Hebrew word **Olam** is used to describe God, it means an infinite duration of existence which alone can measure the life of God. This is **measureless**, eternal!

"Lord, thou hast been our dwelling place in all generations. Before the mountains were brought forth, or ever thou hadst formed the earth and the world, even from everlasting to everlasting, thou art God." Psalm 90:1,2.

This is the first of the mysteries of the Divine Nature.

God Is Changeless

The second fact we need to know is that the eternal God is changeless.

"For I am the Lord, I change not; therefore ye sons of Jacob are not consumed." Mal. 3:6

"Every good gift and every perfect gift is from above, and cometh down from the Father of lights, with whom is no variableness, neither shadow of turning." James 1:17

"Jesus Christ the same yesterday, and to day, and for ever." Heb. 13:8

"Of old hast thou laid the foundation of the earth: and the heavens are the work of thy hands. They shall perish, but thou shalt endure: yea, all of

them shall wax old like a garment; as a vesture shalt thou change them, and they shall be changed: But thou art the same, and thy years shall have no end." Psalm 102:25-27

Changelessness is the essential characteristic of the eternal state. God is timeless and changeless and therefore He is **absolutely eternal** i.e. beginningless and endless.

God is without beginning. God has always existed. Before there was anything else, God had always been in existence. Therefore the only absolute principles of existence are those principles which are inherent or intrinsic in God. And thus the only right ways are God's ways. This brings us, in fact, to the absolute definition of RIGHT. Since God is without beginning and without ending, then the principles of His existence are the only absolutely right principles. It also means that, when God does anything, His way of doing it is the only right way and it is not merely right, it is the only and most excellent and perfect way of doing it.

God Is Infinite In Righteousness

"The Lord is righteous in all his ways, and holy in all his works." Psa. 145:17

"The Lord is good to all: and his tender mercies are over all his works." Psalm 145:9

God Possesses The Infinite Perfect Eternal Life

Only God is inherently immortal.

"Who only hath immortality, dwelling in the light which no man can approach unto; whom no man hath seen, nor can see: to whom be honour and power everlasting. Amen." 1 Tim. 6:16

"For as the Father hath life in himself; so hath he given to the Son to have life in himself;" John 5:26

God Is Omnipotent

"… The LORD GOD Omnipotent reigneth" Rev. 19:6. Within God there is the absolute and infinite concentration of eternal power.

"For the invisible things of him from the creation of the world are clearly seen, being understood by the things that are made, even his eternal power and Godhead; so that they are without excuse:" Romans 1:20.

God Is Infinite In Wisdom And Knowledge

Great is our Lord, and of great power: his understanding is infinite. Psalm 147:5

God knows everything about everything. He knows all the past, all the present and all the future.

Wisdom is the righteous use of power to produce perfect work.

In God there is the eternal application of infinite righteousness to infinite power to eternally produce infinitely perfect excellence and perfect eternal life.

God knows every microscopic detail of everything and He knows how best everything should function.

Neither is there any creature that is not manifest in his sight: but all things are naked and opened unto the eyes of him with whom we have to do. Heb. 4:13.

O the depth of the riches both of the wisdom and knowledge of God! how unsearchable are his judgments, and his ways past finding out! For who hath known the mind of the Lord? or who hath been his counsellor? Or who hath first given to him, and it shall be recompensed unto him again? For of him, and through him, and to him, are all things: to whom be glory for ever. Amen. Romans 11:33-36

He is the Rock, his work is perfect: for all his ways are judgment: a God of truth and without iniquity, just and right is he. Deut. 32:4

The works of the Lord are great, sought out of all them that have pleasure therein. His work is honourable and glorious: and his righteousness endureth for ever. Psalm 111:2,3

God is the absolute eternal TRUTH, and the knowledge of God is absolute truth.

God Is Love

He that loveth not knoweth not God; for God is love. 1 John 4:8.

The love of God (Greek Agape) is not a feeling, it is a principle. God's love is the eternal, unchanging principle by which God uses His power righteously and unselfishly for the good of His creation.

Eternal love is that eternal principle by which infinite wisdom applies infinite righteousness to infinite power for the eternal production of the perfect life and perfect works.

God's Agape love means doing the best for others whatever the cost to oneself.

The supreme demonstration of God's love was given when the Creator took on our human nature and sacrificed Himself to save sinners.

But God commendeth his love toward us, in that, while we were yet sinners, Christ died for us. Rom. 5:8

For God so loved the world, that he gave his only begotten Son, that whosoever believeth in him should not perish, but have everlasting life. John 3:16

The beautiful characteristics of Divine Love are described in 1 Cor. 13:4-8:

"Love is patient; Love is kind and envies no one. Love is never boastful, nor conceited, nor rude; never selfish, not quick to take offence. Love keeps no score of wrongs; does not gloat over other men's sins, but delights in the truth. There is nothing love cannot face; there is no limit to its faith, its hope, and its endurance. Love will never come to an end." 1 Cor. 13:4-8. (TEV)

Love's application of Eternal Wisdom and Eternal Righteousness to Eternal Power is the eternal basis of eternal life, eternal peace, eternal order, eternal joy, eternal security, eternal beauty and eternal freedom. God is therefore the only Source of genuine peace, genuine order, genuine joy, eternal security, infinite beauty and absolute freedom.

God, The Creator

God was not dependent on pre-existent matter when creating the universe. He created matter from nothing by His infinite power, infinite wisdom and infinite love.

By the word of the Lord were the heavens made; and all the host of them by the breath of his mouth. Psalm 33:6.

God created our planet from nothing and then made it into a perfect paradise in six days. Each day God did some special creative work for that day, until He crowned it all off with the creation of mankind on the sixth day. He then rested on the seventh day in celebration of the finishing of a perfect work on earth.

"Thus the heavens and the earth were finished, and all the host of them. And on the seventh day God ended his work which he had made; and he rested on the seventh day from all his work which he had made. And God blessed the seventh day, and sanctified it: because that in it he had rested from all his work which God created and made." Gen. 2:1-3.

God had created the angels by speaking them into existence, but He created man from the substance of the earth. All His intelligent creatures were made free moral agents with freedom of choice to obey or to disobey God's perfect law.

Before the entrance of sin, all creation was absolutely perfect. Sin developed in heaven before the creation of our planet and solar system. The Son of God, who is as eternal as the Father, made all things.

"In the beginning was the Word, and the Word was with God, and the Word was God. The same was in the beginning with God. All things were made by him; and without him was not any thing made that was made.... And the Word was made flesh, and dwelt among us, (and we beheld his glory, the glory as of the only begotten of the Father,) full of grace and truth." John 1:1-3, 14

"For by him were all things created, that are in heaven, and that are in earth, visible and invisible, whether they be thrones, or dominions, or

principalities, or powers: all things were created by him, and for him: And he is before all things, and by him all things consist." Col. 1:16, 17

The proof of the absolute eternity and Godhead of the Son of God is established by the following texts of scripture: (John 8:58; Exodus 3:14); (Isaiah 44:6, Rev. 1:17); (Psalm 102:24-27, Hebrews 1:8-12); (Psalm 90:1,2, Proverbs 8:22,23).

In fact scripture reveals the unfathomable mystery that the Son of God is the **WISDOM,** the **Word** (Greek: *logos*), the Righteousness of God. Therefore the Father does everything through His Son.

"In the beginning was the Word, and the Word was with God, and the Word was God. The same was in the beginning with God. All things were made by him; and without him was not any thing made that was made." John 1:1-3

"Behold, the days come, saith the Lord, that I will raise unto David a righteous Branch, and a King shall reign and prosper, and shall execute judgment and justice in the earth. In his days Judah shall be saved, and Israel shall dwell safely: and this is his name whereby he shall be called, THE LORD OUR RIGHTEOUSNESS." Jeremiah 23:5,6

"But of him are ye in Christ Jesus, who of God is made unto us wisdom, and righteousness, and sanctification, and redemption: That, according as it is written, He that glorieth, let him glory in the Lord." 1 Cor. 1:30,31. (Read also Proverbs 8).

Six

The Origin And Nature Of Sin

Sin was not always in the universe. It was definitely not created or caused by God. Sin developed in the mind of the highest and most honored of the angels. Nothing is more clearly taught in the Bible than that God was in no way responsible for the development of sin or any of its consequences.

> *"He that committeth sin is of the devil; for the devil sinneth from the beginning. For this purpose the Son of God was manifested, that he might destroy the works of the devil. Whosoever is born of God doth not commit sin; for his seed remaineth in him: and he cannot sin, because he is born of God." 1 John 3:8,9*

> *"Let no man say when he is tempted, I am tempted of God: for God cannot be tempted with evil, neither tempteth he any man:" James 1:13*

> *"Another parable put he forth unto them, saying, The kingdom of heaven is likened unto a man which sowed good seed in his field: But while men slept, his enemy came and sowed tares among the wheat, and went his way. But when the blade was sprung up, and brought forth fruit, then appeared the tares also. So the servants of the householder came and said unto him, Sir, didst not thou sow good seed in thy field? from whence then hath it tares? He said unto them, An enemy hath done this. The servants said unto him, Wilt thou then that we go and gather them up?" Matt. 13:24-28*

> *"This then is the message which we have heard of him, and declare unto you, that God is light, and in him is no darkness at all." 1 John 1:5*

"The Lord is righteous in all his ways, and holy in all his works."
Psalm 145:17

"For I am the Lord, I change not; therefore ye sons of Jacob are not consumed." Mal. 3:6

The **basis** of sin is self-exaltation.

"How art thou fallen from heaven, O Lucifer, son of the morning! how art thou cut down to the ground, which didst weaken the nations! For thou hast said in thine heart, I will ascend into heaven, I will exalt my throne above the stars of God: I will sit also upon the mount of the congregation, in the sides of the north: I will ascend above the heights of the clouds; I will be like the most High." Isaiah 14:12-14.

The definition of sin is *"transgression of God's law."* Sin is a principle at war with the principle of unselfish love, which is the foundation of God's Government.

"Whosoever committeth sin transgresseth also the law: for sin is the transgression of the law." 1 John 3:4

"He that loveth not knoweth not God; for God is love." 1 John 4:8

"Love worketh no ill to his neighbour: therefore love is the fulfilling of the law." Rom. 13:10

The definition of sin, then, is "doing things by a way other than by God's way." But since God does everything right, sin means doing things in the wrong way. Sin is unrighteousness in action, it uses power unrighteously. Sin separates righteousness from power and hence perverts the powers of creation into unrighteous destructive powers when not restrained by God's mercy.

The Nature of Sin

It is the nature of sin to separate us from God, to hide God's face from us.

"Behold, the Lord's hand is not shortened, that it cannot save; neither his ear heavy, that it cannot hear: But your iniquities have separated between you and your God, and your sins have hid his face from you, that he will not hear." Isaiah 59:1,2.

Sin is, in fact, asking God to leave us alone, to depart from us.

> *"Which said unto God, Depart from us: and what can the Almighty do for them?" Job. 22:17.*

Since sin separates creature from Creator, it produces death.

> *"Then when lust hath conceived, it bringeth forth sin: and sin, when it is finished, bringeth forth death." James 1:15*

> *"For the wages of sin is death; but the gift of God is eternal life through Jesus Christ our Lord." Rom. 6:23*

> *"The sting of death is sin; and the strength of sin is the law." 1 Cor. 15:56*

Because God is the fountain of life, separation from God by sin produces death.

> *"For with thee is the fountain of life: in thy light shall we see light." Psalm 36:9*

> *"O Lord, the hope of Israel, all that forsake thee shall be ashamed, and they that depart from me shall be written in the earth, because they have forsaken the Lord, the fountain of living waters." Jer. 17:13*

> *"For my people have committed two evils; they have forsaken me the fountain of living waters, and hewed them out cisterns, broken cisterns, that can hold no water." Jer. 2:13*

Sin, then, is malignant, it produces destruction and death because it separates every detail of the structure and function of the affected part of creation from God's righteousness. The Holy Spirit must apply God's wisdom and Righteousness in Christ to every detail of the structure and function of creation in order for created things to be maintained in perfect structural and functional integrity. Sin separates from God and produces destruction and death.

> *"Then when lust hath conceived, it bringeth forth sin: and sin, when it is finished, bringeth forth death." James 1:15*

> *"In the way of righteousness is life; and in the pathway thereof there is no death." Prov. 12:28*

> *"For whoso findeth me findeth life, and shall obtain favour of the Lord. But he that sinneth against me wrongeth his own soul: all they that hate me love death." Prov. 8:35,36.*

As mentioned before, sin originated in heaven in the mind of Lucifer. He opposed the law and the government of God. He declared that his way was better than God's way. The warfare against God, His Government and His law began in heaven.

"And there was war in heaven: Michael and his angels fought against the dragon; and the dragon fought and his angels, And prevailed not; neither was their place found any more in heaven. And the great dragon was cast out, that old serpent, called the Devil, and Satan, which deceiveth the whole world: he was cast out into the earth, and his angels were cast out with him." Revelation 12:7-9

"Moreover, the word of the Lord came unto me, saying, Son of man, take up a lamentation upon the king of Tyrus, and say unto him, Thus saith the Lord God; Thou sealest up the sum, full of wisdom, and perfect in beauty. Thou hast been in Eden the garden of God; every precious stone was thy covering, the sardius, topaz, and the diamond, the beryl, the onyx, and the jasper, the sapphire, the emerald, and the carbuncle, and gold: the workmanship of thy tabrets and of thy pipes was prepared in thee in the day that thou wast created. Thou art the anointed cherub that covereth; and I have set thee so: thou wast upon the holy mountain of God; thou hast walked up and down in the midst of the stones of fire. Thou wast perfect in thy ways from the day that thou wast created, till iniquity was found in thee. By the multitude of thy merchandise they have filled the midst of thee with violence, and thou hast sinned: therefore I will cast thee as profane out of the mountain of God: and I will destroy thee, O covering cherub, from the midst of the stones of fire. Thine heart was lifted up because of thy beauty, thou hast corrupted thy wisdom by reason of thy brightness: I will cast thee to the ground, I will lay thee before kings, that they may behold thee. Thou hast defiled thy sanctuaries by the multitude of thine iniquities, by the iniquity of thy traffick; therefore will I bring forth a fire from the midst of thee, it shall devour thee, and I will bring thee to ashes upon the earth in the sight of all them that behold thee. All they that know thee among the people shall be astonished at thee: thou shalt be a terror, and never shalt thou be any more." Ezekial 28:11-19

"Whosoever committeth sin transgresseth also the law: for sin is the transgression of the law... He that committeth sin is of the devil; for the devil sinneth from the beginning. For this purpose the Son of God was manifested, that he might destroy the works of the devil." 1 John 3:4,8

Satan deceived one third of the angels. He did this by telling lies on God's character, government and law.

> *"Ye are of your father the devil, and the lusts of your father ye will do. He was a murderer from the beginning, and abode not in the truth, because there is no truth in him. When he speaketh a lie, he speaketh of his own: for he is a liar, and the father of it." John 8:44*

Satan was the first creature to suggest that God's law was burdensome or grievous and that it ought not to be obeyed. But God declares that His commandments are not grievous.

> *"For this is the love of God, that we keep his commandments: and his commandments are not grievous." 1 John 5:3.*

The parable of the talents in Matthew 25 also reveals some of the other falsehoods or lies which Satan told against God's character.

> *"Then he which had received the one talent came and said, Lord, I knew thee that thou art an hard man, reaping where thou hast not sown, and gathering where thou hast not strawed: And I was afraid, and went and hid thy talent in the earth: lo, there thou hast that is thine." Matt. 25:24,25.*

Satan has charged that God is a tyrant (a hard God), that He is selfish, arbitrary, severe, and that He seeks His own aggrandizement while oppressing His creatures. Satan therefore asserts that creatures should be afraid of God.

But perhaps the most dangerous falsehood told by Satan was told to the human race through Adam and Eve. God had informed our first parents that disobedience—sin—would produce death. Satan countered by telling them that they would not die, that seeking their own way would be harmless.

> *"But of the tree of the knowledge of good and evil, thou shalt not eat of it: for in the day that thou eatest thereof thou shalt surely die." Gen. 2:17*

> *"Now the serpent was more subtle than any beast of the field which the Lord God had made. And he said unto the woman, Yea, hath God said, Ye shall not eat of every tree of the garden? And the woman said unto the serpent, We may eat of the fruit of the trees of the garden: But of the fruit of the tree which is in the midst of the garden, God hath said, Ye shall not eat of it, neither shall ye touch it, lest ye die. And the serpent said unto the woman, Ye shall not surely die:" Gen. 3:1-4*

Thus Satan has deceived the whole world into believing that 'ownwayness', which is sin, does not produce death.

As a result people blame everything else, except sin, for death. They especially blame God. The majority of people, even religious people, believe that the only problem with sin is that it makes God angry and causes Him to kill sinners. And many more believe that sinners will not die at all but will live forever in hell-fire. Indeed Satan has deceived the whole world.

> *"And the great dragon was cast out, that old serpent, called the Devil, and Satan, which deceiveth the whole world: he was cast out into the earth, and his angels were cast out with him." Rev. 12:9.*

So far, then, we see that sin transgresses God's law, opposes God's Government, separates from God and ultimately, whenever it is finished, produces death. Sin is the root cause of all the sickness, disease, accidents, natural calamities, crime, lawlessness, destruction and death in the world.

Sin started in Heaven and entered our world when Adam and Eve gave in to Satan's temptation.

> *"Wherefore, as by one man sin entered into the world, and death by sin; and so death passed upon all men, for that all have sinned:" Rom. 5:12.*

Furthermore in order to establish his government of sin, Satan has promulgated lies about God's character and he has blackened God's reputation. That was why Jesus had to come to give us the revelation written down in 1 John 1:5.

> *"This then is the message which we have heard of him, and declare unto you, that God is light, and in him is no darkness at all." 1 John 1:5.*

Yes friend, God is light and in Him is no darkness at all, therefore God cannot and can never be the source of sin or evil or death.

He is the fountain of life.

It is sin which causes separation from God and therefore produces all evil and ultimately produces death.

The sin problem which started in Heaven is now localized on our planet. The onlooking universe has watched, is watching and will watch the ongoing saga, i.e. the great controversy between God and Satan.

God claims that no other way but His can work. He has warned that sin is the root cause of all the problems, all the evil and all the death in our world. He has declared that only His way of selfless love, truth, wisdom and righteousness can conquer sin and produce eternal peace.

Satan has charged that creatures can be happy and successful in their own way apart from God's way. Satan declares that sin does not produce death, and blames God for sin, its evil results, and death.

Who is telling the truth?

Can God be trusted? Has He been telling us the truth? The falsehoods which Satan has promulgated have so deceived men and angels that God's name and government must be cleared, justified and vindicated. The Heavenly Sanctuary is representative of God's government.

The prophet Daniel informs us that the work of cleansing the Heavenly Sanctuary was to commence at the end of the 2300 prophetic days of Daniel 8:14. The cleansing of the Heavenly Sanctuary refers to the work of vindicating and clearing God's name, character and reputation from the false charges Satan and man have laid against God.

In order to cleanse the Heavenly Sanctuary, God's people must reach the point where they so hate sin and love righteousness that they will make the victorious righteousness of Christ their own experience, and thereby willingly and lovingly obey the law of love perfectly. At the same time they will manifest the harmlessness of God's ways by loving and forgiving their enemies as Jesus did on the cross.

By obeying God without the slightest deviation even in the face of death, and by loving and forgiving their enemies, THEY WILL PROVE SATAN WRONG AND GOD RIGHT and win the last battle in the long-standing conflict between light and darkness.

Seven

The Wrath Of God

The Bible leaves us in no doubt that God hates sin, and He abhors evil. It also leaves us in no doubt that God is not the source or cause of evil. There is no evil in God. In fact, God so hates sin that He cannot even look at it.

> "Thou hast loved righteousness, and hated iniquity; therefore God, even thy God, hath anointed thee with the oil of gladness above thy fellows." Hebrews 1:9

> "Let no man say when he is tempted, I am tempted of God: for God cannot be tempted with evil, neither tempteth he any man: But every man is tempted, when he is drawn away of his own lust, and enticed. Then when lust hath conceived, it bringeth forth sin: and sin, when it is finished, bringeth forth death. Do not err, my beloved brethren. Every good gift and every perfect gift is from above, and cometh down from the Father of lights, with whom is no variableness, neither shadow of turning." James 1:13-17

> "The Lord is righteous in all his ways, and holy in all his works." Psa. 145:17

> "This then is the message which we have heard of him, and declare unto you, that God is light, and in him is no darkness at all. If we say that we have fellowship with him, and walk in darkness, we lie, and do not the truth:" 1 John 1 :5,6

> "He that committeth sin is of the devil; for the devil sinneth from the beginning. For this purpose the Son of God was manifested, that he might

destroy the works of the devil... In this the children of God are manifest, and the children of the devil: whosoever doeth not righteousness is not of God, neither he that loveth not his brother." 1 John 3 :8,10.

Why does God hate sin? God hates sin because sin separates His creatures from Him and thereby destroys them:

"But your iniquities have separated between you and your God, and your sins have hid his face from you, that he will not hear." Isaiah 59:2

"Evil shall slay the wicked: and they that hate the righteous shall be desolate." Psalm 34:21

"For the Lord knoweth the way of the righteous: but the way of the ungodly shall perish." Psalm 1:6

Sin is telling God to depart. And God knows, and we need to know too, that when He departs the end-result is destruction:

"Hast thou marked the old way which wicked men have trodden? Which were cut down out of time, whose foundation was overflown with a flood: Which said unto God, Depart from us: and what can the Almighty do for them?" Job. 22:15-17

"O Lord, the hope of Israel, all that forsake thee shall be ashamed, and they that depart from me shall be written in the earth, because they have forsaken the Lord, the fountain of living waters." Jer. 17:13

"And the destruction of the transgressors and of the sinners shall be together, and they that forsake the Lord shall be consumed." Isaiah 1:28

Going back now to Isaiah 59:2 we see clearly that sin separates between creature and Creator and hides His face from His creatures:

"Behold, the Lord's hand is not shortened, that it cannot save; neither his ear heavy, that it cannot hear: But your iniquities have separated between you and your God, and your sins have hid his face from you, that he will not hear." Isaiah 59:1,2

Furthermore Isaiah 54:7-8 defines the mechanism of wrath as the hiding of God's face:

"In a little wrath I hid my face from thee for a moment; but with everlasting kindness will I have mercy on thee, saith the Lord thy Redeemer." Isaiah 54:8

"How long, Lord? wilt thou hide thyself for ever? shall thy wrath burn like fire?" Psalm 89:46

"Hide not thy face far from me; put not thy servant away in anger: thou hast been my help; leave me not, neither forsake me, O God of my salvation." Psalm 27:9

"Lord, by thy favour thou hast made my mountain to stand strong: thou didst hide thy face, and I was troubled." Psalm 30:7

"Hear me speedily, O Lord: my spirit faileth: hide not thy face from me, lest I be like unto them that go down into the pit." Psalm 143:7

Now how does God exercise His wrath? Perhaps the clearest New Testament answer (other than the Sacrifice of Jesus Christ) was given by Paul in Romans 1:18 where he states clearly that the wrath of God is revealed from Heaven against all sin:

"For the wrath of God is revealed from heaven against all ungodliness and unrighteousness of men, who hold the truth in unrighteousness;" Rom. 1:18

In Romans 1:19-23 Paul shows that there is no excuse for sin or godlessnesss. Then in verse 24 he also explains how God exercises wrath. Paul states in Romans 1:24.

"WHEREFORE GOD ALSO GAVE THEM UP ...."

Paul repeats this explanation in verse 26

"FOR THIS CAUSE GOD GAVE THEM UP...."

and in verse 28

"... GOD GAVE THEM OVER...."

Paul is clear in Romans 1:18-28 that God excercises His wrath by "giving up" the sinner to reap the consequences of sin.

But where did Paul get this explanation from? The only scriptures available in his day were the scriptures of the Old Testament.

Can we find this explanation in the Old Testament? Yes!

Wrath, in all its various linguistic descriptions, was inflicted upon Israel and Judah regularly in the Old Testament Era.

In Deuteronomy chapter 28, God, through Moses, had given to the Israelites a list of the blessings of obedience (Deut. 28:1-15), and a very much longer list of the curses of disobedience (Deut. 28:15-68).

Let us now examine the language used to describe the curses, as we examine some of the verses in Deut. 28:15-68:Consider these verses.

> *"The Lord shall send upon thee cursing, vexation, and rebuke, in all that thou settest thine hand unto for to do, until thou be destroyed, and until thou perish quickly; because of the wickedness of thy doings, whereby thou hast forsaken me.The Lord shall make the pestilence cleave unto thee, until he have consumed thee from off the land, whither thou goest to possess it. The Lord shall smite thee with a consumption, and with a fever, and with an inflammation, and with an extreme burning, and with the sword, and with blasting, and with mildew; and they shall pursue thee until thou perish.*
>
> *The Lord will smite thee with the botch of Egypt, and with the emerods, and with the scab, and with the itch, whereof thou canst not be healed. The Lord shall smite thee with madness, and blindness, and astonishment of heart:*
>
> *Then the Lord will make thy plagues wonderful, and the plagues of thy seed, even great plagues, and of long continuance, and sore sicknesses, and of long continuance. Moreover, he will bring upon thee all the diseases of Egypt, which thou wast afraid of; and they shall cleave unto thee. Also every sickness, and every plague, which is not written in the book of this law, them will the Lord bring upon thee, until thou be destroyed." Deut. 28:20-22,27-28,59-61.*

Each of these texts describes Israel's punishment as striking them by a direct decree or a direct act of God. But wait a minute! Let us turn in our Bibles to Deuteronomy Chapter 31 verses 16-18:

> *"And the Lord said unto Moses, Behold, thou shalt sleep with thy fathers; and this people will rise up, and go a whoring after the gods of the strangers of the land, whither they go to be among them, and will forsake me, and break my covenant which I have made with them. Then my*

anger shall be kindled against them in that day, and I will forsake them, and I will hide my face from them, and they shall be devoured, and many evils and troubles shall befall them; so that they will say in that day, Are not these evils come upon us, because our God is not among us? And I will surely hide my face in that day for all the evils which they shall have wrought, in that they are turned unto other gods." Deut. 31:16-18.

Verse 17 explains very clearly the meaning and mechanism of wrath. When the Israelites forsook God by rejecting His loving invitations and warnings, He forsook them, His face was hid from them and all the evils which befell them happened because God was not among them.

It is very clear then that the mechanism of God's wrath is the separation caused by sin. It is this separation between God and sinners that produces the "punishment." For futher confirmation refer to the following texts:

"Evil shall slay the wicked: and they that hate the righteous shall be desolate." Psalm 34:21

"But your iniquities have separated between you and your God, and your sins have hid his face from you, that he will not hear." Isaiah 59:2

"Let no man say when he is tempted, I am tempted of God: for God cannot be tempted with evil, neither tempteth he any man: But every man is tempted, when he is drawn away of his own lust, and enticed. Then when lust hath conceived, it bringeth forth sin: and sin, when it is finished, bringeth forth death." James 1:13-15

"Then my anger shall be kindled against them in that day, and I will forsake them, and I will hide my face from them, and they shall be devoured, and many evils and troubles shall befall them; so that they will say in that day, Are not these evils come upon us, because our God is not among us?" Deut. 31:17

The punishments do not come by the direct decreee or direct infliction by God. NO! The punishments come from sin itself as it separates from God.

The problem with us is that we try to understand God's wrath in terms of human wrath, but this is one thing we should never do. The reason is written down in James 1:20:

"For the wrath of man worketh not the righteousness of God." James 1:20

Human wrath transgresses God's law and therefore is sin. God's wrath is righteous—it does not act contrary to God's law of love. God exercises His wrath by giving up those who reject Him. This "giving up" may be partial or complete as we shall learn from later studies. To further clarify this point, consider Hosea 11:7-9:

> "And my people are bent to backsliding from me: though they called them to the most High, none at all would exalt him. How shall I give thee up, Ephraim? how shall I deliver thee, Israel? how shall I make thee as Admah? how shall I set thee as Zeboim? mine heart is turned within me, my repentings are kindled together. I will not execute the fierceness of mine anger, I will not return to destroy Ephraim: for I am God, and not man; the Holy One in the midst of thee: and I will not enter into the city." Hosea 11:7-9.

God asked His ancient people a question in Hosea 11:8, "HOW SHALL I GIVE THEE UP, EPHRAIM? How shall I deliver thee Israel?"

And notice in verse 8 that in giving them up He would be making them as Admah and Zeboim, cities of the plain, which were destroyed with Sodom and Gomorrah (See Genesis 14:2; 19:24, 25). This principle in these verses will be important in our understanding of the flood and who/what brought about the flood. But understand from verse 9 that His giving them up was equivalent to:

- executing the fierceness of His anger and
- destroying them.

Hosea 11:7-9 then establishes the following identity of meanings:

God's Wrath = His Giving Them Up = The Execution Of His Fierce Anger = His Destroying Them

And remember Isaiah 59:2 and 54:8 which explain that God's wrath is the hiding of His face caused by sin. It is the terrible separation, caused by sin, which produces destruction according to the principles of Jeremiah 17:13 and James 1:13-15.

Another term employed in scripture to describe wrath is the term *HE SPARED NOT.* Consider 2 Peter 2 verses 4-6:

> "For if God spared not the angels that sinned, but cast them down to hell, and delivered them into chains of darkness, to be reserved unto

judgment; And spared not the old world, but saved Noah the eighth person, a preacher of righteousness, bringing in the flood upon the world of the ungodly; And turning the cities of Sodom and Gomorrha into ashes condemned them with an overthrow, making them an ensample unto those that after should live ungodly;" 2 Peter 2:4,5,6.

We now come to a crucial point. Jesus suffered the wrath of God for us.

"For he hath made him to be sin for us, who knew no sin; that we might be made the righteousness of God in him."2 Cor. 5:21

"What shall we then say to these things? If God be for us, who can be against us? He that spared not his own Son, but delivered him up for us all, how shall he not with him also freely give us all things?" *Romans 8:31, 32*

God **spared not** the angels who sinned.
God **spared not** the pre-flood world.
God **spared not** the cities of the plain: Sodom, Gomorrah, Admah, Zeboim.
God **spared not** His Son!

"Surely he hath borne our griefs, and carried our sorrows: yet we did esteem him stricken, smitten of God, and afflicted. But he was wounded for our transgressions, he was bruised for our iniquities: the chastisement of our peace was upon him; and with his stripes we are healed. All we like sheep have gone astray; we have turned every one to his own way; and the Lord hath laid on him the iniquity of us all." Isaiah 53:4-6.

Now the critical question: Will He spare us? Yes, but only in Christ!

"Therefore we ought to give the more earnest heed to the things which we have heard, lest at any time we should let them slip. For if the word spoken by angels was stedfast, and every transgression and disobedience received a just recompence of reward; How shall we escape, if we neglect so great salvation; which at the first began to be spoken by the Lord, and was confirmed unto us by them that heard him;" Heb. 2:1-3.

Eight

The Cross Reveals The Mechanism Of Divine Punishment

> *"What shall we then say to these things? If God be for us, who can be against us? He that spared not his own Son, but delivered him up for us all, how shall he not with him also freely give us all things?" Romans 8:31-32*

Jesus was **not spared**, He was **given up** for us all.

In order to be our Substitute and Surety Jesus had to suffer the **full** punishment of sin for **all** mankind. God His Father could **not** spare Him in **any way.** God had to treat Him in the **same** way that the unrepentant sinner will be treated in the day of executive judgement.

> *"For he hath made him to be sin for us, who knew no sin; that we might be made the righteousness of God in him." 2 Cor. 5:21*

> *"But your iniquities have separated between you and your God, and your sins have hid his face from you, that he will not hear." Isaiah 59:2*

> *"For the wages of sin is death.."Romans 6:23 first part*

> *"But we see Jesus, who was made a little lower than the angels for the suffering of death, crowned with glory and honour; that he by the grace of God should taste death for every man." Hebrews 2:9*

Jesus bore the punishment which was our just due. He had to suffer the full wrath of God against sin for us.

> *"Surely he hath borne our griefs, and carried our sorrows: yet we did esteem him stricken, smitten of God, and afflicted. But he was wounded for our transgressions, he was bruised for our iniquities: the chastisement*

of our peace was upon him; and with his stripes we are healed. All we like sheep have gone astray; we have turned every one to his own way; and the Lord hath laid on him the iniquity of us all...

Yet it pleased the Lord to bruise him; he hath put him to grief: when thou shalt make his soul an offering for sin, he shall see his seed, he shall prolong his days, and the pleasure of the Lord shall prosper in his hand." Isaiah 53:4-6, 10.

The Bible speaks of two deaths, first and second. The first is the death of the body and the unconscious sleep of the soul. The second death is destruction of body and soul in the final executive judgement.

"And fear not them which kill the body, but are not able to kill the soul: but rather fear him which is able to destroy both soul and body in hell." Matthew 10:28

"These things said he: and after that he saith unto them, Our friend Lazarus sleepeth; but I go, that I may awake him out of sleep. Then said his disciples, Lord, if he sleep, he shall do well. Howbeit Jesus spake of his death: but they thought that he had spoken of taking of rest in sleep. Then said Jesus unto them plainly, Lazarus is dead. And I am glad for your sakes that I was not there, to the intent ye may believe; nevertheless let us go unto him." John 11:11-15

"He that overcometh shall inherit all things; and I will be his God, and he shall be my son. But the fearful, and unbelieving, and the abominable, and murderers, and whoremongers, and sorcerers, and idolaters, and all liars, shall have their part in the lake which burneth with fire and brimstone: which is the second death." Rev. 21:7,8

Both the first and the second deaths are caused by sin.

"Wherefore, as by one man sin entered into the world, and death by sin; and so death passed upon all men, for that all have sinned:" Romans 5:12

"For the wages of sin is death; but the gift of God is eternal life through Jesus Christ our Lord." Romans 6:23

"Then when lust hath conceived, it bringeth forth sin: and sin, when it is finished, bringeth forth death." James 1:15

Jesus therefore had to taste, experience and die both deaths in order to be our complete Substitute, Surety and Saviour.

> *"But we see Jesus, who was made a little lower than the angels for the suffering of death, crowned with glory and honour; that he by the grace of God should taste death for every man." Hebrews 2:9.*

Satan inspired the Jews and Romans to kill Jesus' body. The sins of the whole world separated His soul from God thereby inflicting the second death upon Him.

> *"Therefore will I divide him a portion with the great, and he shall divide the spoil with the strong; because he hath poured out his soul unto death: and he was numbered with the transgressors; and he bare the sin of many, and made intercession for the transgressors." Isaiah 53:12*

By examining carefully how Jesus died on the cross, we shall be able to understand the mechanism by which God's wrath, His fierce anger, His justice, His punishing, His smiting, His destroying the sinner, operates!

In the Garden of Gethsemane Jesus began to experience the terrible separation which the weight of all the sins of the whole world would cause. In words of burning anguish He uttered:

> *"My soul is exceeding sorrowful, even unto death: tarry ye here and watch with me." Matt. 26:38.*

As the anguish increased He fell on His face and prayed

> *"And he went a little farther, and fell on his face, and prayed, saying, O my Father, if it be possible, let this cup pass from me: nevertheless not as I will, but as thou wilt. And he cometh unto the disciples, and findeth them asleep, and saith unto Peter, What, could ye not watch with me one hour? Watch and pray, that ye enter not into temptation: the spirit indeed is willing, but the flesh is weak. He went away again the second time, and prayed, saying, O my Father, if this cup may not pass away from me, except I drink it, thy will be done." Matt. 26:39-42.*

In fact Mark indicates that He prayed three times in all. (See Mark 14:41). At last His mind was fixed, He would save mankind at any cost to Himself. What infinite love!

During His "trial" He clearly stated that no man could have had any power to hurt Him unless the Father had "given Him up."

"Then saith Pilate unto him, Speakest thou not unto me? knowest thou not that I have power to crucify thee, and have power to release thee? Jesus answered, Thou couldest have no power at all against me, except it were given thee from above: therefore he that delivered me unto thee hath the greater sin." John 19:10-11.

This is what Paul meant in Romans 4:25 and in Romans 8:32.

"Who was delivered for our offences, and was raised again for our justification."Romans 4:25.

"He that spared not his own Son, but delivered him up for us all, how shall he not with him also freely give us all things?" Romans 8:32.

Yes! God the Father did not spare His Son but delivered Him up. God gave Jesus up to the terrible consequences of sin.

"Christ hath redeemed us from the curse of the law, being made a curse for us: for it is written, Cursed is every one that hangeth on a tree:" Gal. 3:13

At the physical level His enemies tortured His body and heaped ridicule upon His mind.

At the spiritual level, the iniquity of the whole world was laid upon Jesus and separated His entire being from God, thereby producing the sufferings and actuality of the second death. As Jesus experienced the terrible separation which sin causes between the soul and God, He cried out: (Matthew 27:46)

"My god, my god, why hast thou forsaken me?"

Please read the whole of Psalm 22.

Question: **What killed Jesus?**
Answer: **The sins of the whole world separated Him from God the Father and killed Him. Our sins hid His Father's face from Christ. The Father forsook His Son.**

"For he hath made him to be sin for us, who knew no sin; that we might be made the righteousness of God in him." 2 Cor. 5:21

"Therefore will I divide him a portion with the great, and he shall divide the spoil with the strong; because he hath poured out his soul unto death:

and he was numbered with the transgressors; and he bare the sin of many, and made intercession for the transgressors." Isaiah 53:12

"But your iniquities have separated between you and your God, and your sins have hid his face from you, that he will not hear." Isaiah 59:2

"In a little wrath I hid my face from thee for a moment; but with everlasting kindness will I have mercy on thee, saith the Lord thy Redeemer." Isaiah 54:8

"And about the ninth hour Jesus cried with a loud voice, saying, Eli, Eli, lama sabachthani? that is to say, My God, my God, why hast thou forsaken me?" Matt. 27:46

Our Lord Jesus suffered the hiding of His Father's face. He suffered the wrath of God for us!

The cross therefore confirms the truth that sin produces death by separation from God.

The cross proves that sin whenever it is finished produces death.

The cross proves God right when He said that sin produces death.

The cross proves Satan wrong when he asserted that sin does not cause death.

The cross proves that we all have a genuine choice in the great conflict between light and darkness.

If we choose righteousness we are choosing eternal life.

If we choose unrighteousness we are choosing the second death, and it is sin itself which will destroy us.

"Evil shall slay the wicked: and they that hate the righteous shall be desolate." Psalm 34:21

"For the wages of sin is death; but the gift of God is eternal life through Jesus Christ our Lord." Romans 6:23

"O Lord, the hope of Israel, all that forsake thee shall be ashamed, and they that depart from me shall be written in the earth, because they have forsaken the Lord, the fountain of living waters." Jer. 17:13

Nine

Lessons From The Book Of Job

We have already learned that, notwithstanding the language of the Old Testament, a careful search of the Bible reveals passages of scripture which contain the principles of correct interpretation by which the mechanism underlying the execution of Divine Judgements may be understood.

One such passage, indeed an entire Book of the Bible, is the Book of Job, which was written by Moses to explain the mechanism underlying this principle. The account begins with a description of Job, his character, his possessions and his concern for his children's salvation. There can be no doubt about Job's loyalty to God and to righteousness.

> "There was a man in the land of Uz, whose name was Job; and that man was perfect and upright, and one that feared God, and eschewed evil. And there were born unto him seven sons and three daughters. His substance also was seven thousand sheep, and three thousand camels, and five hundred yoke of oxen, and five hundred she asses, and a very great household; so that this man was the greatest of all the men of the east. And his sons went and feasted in their houses, every one his day; and sent and called for their three sisters to eat and to drink with them. And it was so, when the days of their feasting were gone about, that Job sent and sanctified them, and rose up early in the morning, and offered burned offerings according to the number of them all: for Job said, It may be that my sons have sinned, and cursed God in their hearts. Thus did Job continually." Job 1:1-5.

At this point the scene changes. There is a special meeting of special persons with God. Strangely enough Satan is present.

"Now there was a day when the sons of God came to present themselves before the Lord, and Satan came also among them." Job 1:6.

God asks Satan some questions.

"And the Lord said unto Satan, Hast thou considered my servant Job, that there is none like him in the earth, a perfect and an upright man, one that feareth God, and escheweth evil?" Job. 1:8.

Satan's answer is a malicious one. He implies that Job is serving God merely for the rewards and not because of any genuine love for righteousness.

"Then Satan answered the Lord, and said, Doth Job fear God for nought? Hast not thou made an hedge about him, and about his house, and about all that he hath on every side? thou hast blessed the work of his hands, and his substance is increased in the land." Job 1:9,10.

Now comes the crucial moment. Satan challenges God over Job!

"But put forth thine hand now, and touch all that he hath, and he will curse thee to thy face." Job. 1:11

Pay careful attention to the language. Satan tells God to put forth His hand and touch all Job's possessions. Let us see now how God "puts forth" His hand "to touch" Job's possessions.

"And the Lord said unto Satan, Behold, all that he hath is in thy power; only upon himself put not forth thine hand. So Satan went forth from the presence of the Lord." Job. 1:12.

It is clearly seen that the way God puts forth His hand to touch Job's possessions is by handing them over, giving them up, to Satan and permitting Satan to destroy them. Notice too that God does not "hand over" Job's body to Satan's power at this time. Soon after God "put forth His hand and touched Job's possessions", meaning, soon after God handed over Job's possessions to Satan, a series of disasters strikes Job.

"And there was a day when his sons and his daughters were eating and drinking wine in their eldest brother's house: And there came a messenger unto Job, and said, The oxen were plowing, and the asses feeding beside them: And the Sabeans fell upon them, and took them away; yea, they have slain the servants with the edge of the sword; and I only am escaped alone to tell thee. While he was yet speaking, there came also another, and said, The fire of God is fallen from heaven, and hath burned up the

sheep, and the servants, and consumed them; and I only am escaped alone to tell thee. While he was yet speaking, there came also another, and said, The Chaldeans made out three bands, and fell upon the camels, and have carried them away, yea, and slain the servants with the edge of the sword; and I only am escaped alone to tell thee. While he was yet speaking, there came also another, and said, Thy sons and thy daughters were eating and drinking wine in their eldest brother's house: And, behold, there came a great wind from the wilderness, and smote the four corners of the house, and it fell upon the young men, and they are dead; and I only am escaped alone to tell thee." Job 1:13-19.

Let us list the calamities which strike Job.

1. Enemies, called the Sabeans, attack and take away all his oxen and donkeys and kill the attendants.

2. The fire of God falls from heaven and burns up sheep and servants.

3. Another set of enemies, called the Chaldeans, kill the servants attending the camels and steals the camels.

4. A wind-storm destroys the house where Job's children are assembled and kills all ten children and their attending servants.

Next is described Job's reaction to the horrible news.

"Then Job arose, and rent his mantle, and shaved his head, and fell down upon the ground, and worshipped, And said, Naked came I out of my mother's womb, and naked shall I return thither: the Lord gave, and the Lord hath taken away; blessed be the name of the Lord. In all this Job sinned not, nor charged God foolishly." Job 1:20-22.

Notice the language in verse 21, *"The Lord gave and the Lord hath taken away..."* But how did the LORD take away? The LORD **"took away"** His possessions by **permitting** Satan to destroy them. Job Chapter 2 opens with another meeting of the sons of God and Satan is among them again. And again God asks him some questions about Job.

"Again there was a day when the sons of God came to present themselves before the Lord, and Satan came also among them to present himself before the Lord. And the Lord said unto Satan, From whence comest

thou? And Satan answered the Lord, and said, From going to and fro in the earth, and from walking up and down in it. And the Lord said unto Satan, Hast thou considered my servant Job, that there is none like him in the earth, a perfect and an upright man, one that feareth God, and escheweth evil? and still he holdeth fast his integrity, although thou movedst me against him, to destroy him without cause." Job 2:1-3.

Notice again the language at the end of verse 3 where God says that Satan moved Him (God) to destroy Job without cause! Obviously the term "God destroyed him without cause" means God **permitted** Satan to destroy him without cause. Well, Satan challenges God again, and God takes up the challenge! He hands over Job's body, but not his life, into Satan's hand.

"And Satan answered the Lord, and said, Skin for skin, yea, all that a man hath will he give for his life. But put forth thine hand now, and touch his bone and his flesh, and he will curse thee to thy face. And the Lord said unto Satan, Behold, he is in thine hand; but save his life." Job 2:4-6.

Satan goes forth from God's presence and smites Job with horrible skin boils from head to foot.

"So went Satan forth from the presence of the Lord, and smote Job with sore boils from the sole of his foot unto his crown. And he took him a potsherd to scrape himself withal; and he sat down among the ashes." Job. 2:7-8.

It is at this point that others, namely his wife and three special friends, are brought into the picture. First, his wife tells him to let go his righteousness and his loyalty to God.

"Then said his wife unto him, Dost thou still retain thine integrity? curse God, and die." Job. 2:9.

Job maintains his commitment and loyalty to God and His righteousness. He rebukes his wife for her folly.

"But he said unto her, Thou speakest as one of the foolish women speaketh. What? shall we receive good at the hand of God, and shall we not receive evil? In all this did not Job sin with his lips." Job. 2:10.

Notice again the language in verse 10, *"What? Shall we receive good at the hand of God, and shall we not receive evil?"* But how did Job receive evil from the hand of God? God permitted Satan's government of sin to strike Job with evil.

Job 2:11 introduces Job's three friends who come to comfort him.

"Now when Job's three friends heard of all this evil that was come upon him, they came every one from his own place; Eliphaz the Temanite, and Bildad the Shuhite, and Zophar the Naamathite: for they had made an appointment together to come to mourn with him and to comfort him." Job. 2:11.

When Job's three friends heard of all the evil that came upon him, they came...

Note carefully that all the calamities which befell Job are called evil. This is a very interesting point because we know that God is never the source of evil. God never does evil, He only permits it.

In the ensuing chapters (8-37) Job and his three friends talk to each other concerning the evil which befell Job. The three friends have good logic and make excellent points but they all miss the crucial and central issue in the story of Job.

Job's friends argue that Job must have sinned otherwise such evil could not have come upon him. His friends assert that God is punishing Job because he has done some secret sin.

Job maintains that he has not departed from God by any sin.

Eventually God speaks (Chapters 38-41) to Job. He simply asks Job certain questions to show how finite we are and how infinite He is. Job's answer to God is one of submissive repentance.

"Wherefore I abhor myself, and repent in dust and ashes." Job 42:6.

God rebukes Job's friends for not saying the right thing about Him. And after Job intercedes for them, God turns the captivity of Job and gives him twice as much as he had before.

"And the Lord turned the captivity of Job, when he prayed for his friends: also the Lord gave Job twice as much as he had before. Then came there unto him all his brethren, and all his sisters, and all they that had been of his acquaintance before, and did eat bread with him in his house: and they bemoaned him, and comforted him over all the evil that the Lord had brought upon him: every man also gave him a piece of money, and every one an earring of gold. So the Lord blessed the latter end of Job more than his beginning: for he had fourteen thousand sheep, and six

thousand camels, and a thousand yoke of oxen, and a thousand she asses. He had also seven sons and three daughters. And he called the name of the first, Jemima; and the name of the second, Kezia; and the name of the third, Kerenhappuch. And in all the land were no women found so fair as the daughters of Job: and their father gave them inheritance among their brethren. After this lived Job an hundred and forty years, and saw his sons, and his sons' sons, even four generations. So Job died, being old and full of days." Job 42:10-17.

Notice again the language of Job 42:11. His relatives and friends comforted him concerning "all the evil the LORD had brought upon him."

How had God brought evil upon Job? By handing him over to, and permitting Satan to afflict him with evil.

The history of Job is very important. It was generally believed by ancient peoples including the Jews that every affliction by God upon an individual (or family) was the penalty of some wrong doing, either of the victim or of his or her parents. Thus the way was prepared for the Jews to reject Jesus. He who "hath borne our griefs and carried our sorrows" was looked upon by the Jews as *"stricken, smitten of God, and afflicted;"* and they looked upon Him with scorn and contempt. (Isaiah 53:3,4).

It was Satan, the author of sin and all its results, who had led men to look upon disease and death as proceeding from God, as punishment arbitrarily inflicted on account of sin. But the history of Job shows that suffering is inflicted by Satan, and is overruled by God for purposes of mercy.

Moreover, the history of Job also teaches us that God permits Satan to bring adversity upon true Christians in order to answer certain charges and prove certain points in the great controversy between God and Satan.

God must demonstrate that His people will remain loyal to His government in spite of all the pressure which Satan can apply.

Furthermore such adversity, permitted by God but caused by Satan, always refines and further seals God's people in their commitment to God and His righteousness.

Ten

The Curse

"Therefore hath the curse devoured the earth and they that dwell therein are desolate: therefore the inhabitants of the earth are burned and few men left." Isaiah 24:6.

This text in Isaiah points forward to the ultimate end-time global results of the curse. But in order to understand the nature of the curse we need to study how it all started. After Adam and Eve disobeyed God and obeyed Satan, sin entered the human family and the world.

"Wherefore, as by one man sin entered into the world, and death by sin; and so death passed upon all men, for that all have sinned:" Romans 5:12.

You can read the account of the fall of mankind in Genesis Chapter 3:14-19 in your own Bible, which describes God as the One who pronounced a **curse** upon the serpent, the woman, the man and also the earth itself.

"And the Lord God said unto the serpent, Because thou hast done this, thou art cursed above all cattle, and above every beast of the field; upon thy belly shalt thou go, and dust shalt thou eat all the days of thy life: And I will put enmity between thee and the woman, and between thy seed and her seed; it shall bruise thy head, and thou shalt bruise his heel. Unto the woman he said, I will greatly multiply thy sorrow and thy conception; in sorrow thou shalt bring forth children; and thy desire shall be to thy husband, and he shall rule over thee. And unto Adam he said, Because thou hast hearkened unto the voice of thy wife, and hast eaten of the tree, of which I commanded thee, saying, Thou shalt not eat of it: cursed is the ground for thy sake; in sorrow shalt thou eat of it all the days of thy life;

Thorns also and thistles shall it bring forth to thee; and thou shalt eat the herb of the field; In the sweat of thy face shalt thou eat bread, till thou return unto the ground; for out of it wast thou taken: for dust thou art, and unto dust shalt thou return." Genesis 3:14-19.

The language of this passage describes God as the One who, by direct decree or direct action, inflicted the curse upon the serpent, the woman, the man and the earth. But, by now, the reader should clearly understand how to interpret such language!

We have already (Chapter 8) studied the list of curses in Deuteronomy 28:15-68 and the mechanism by which such curses come in Deuteronomy 31:16-18.

The pain of childbirth, the curse on the ground causing it to produce thorns and thistles, as well as all the other curses, all resulted from sin separating our planet from God's perfect government. Thorns, thistles, tares and poisonous plants were never made by our loving Creator. We can be sure of this by reading Genesis 1:31. At the end of creation-week God pronounced everything "very good!" Jesus also told a parable which sheds light on this matter in Matthew 13:24-30:

"Another parable put he forth unto them, saying, The kingdom of heaven is likened unto a man which sowed good seed in his field: But while men slept, his enemy came and sowed tares among the wheat, and went his way. But when the blade was sprung up, and brought forth fruit, then appeared the tares also. So the servants of the householder came and said unto him, Sir, didst not thou sow good seed in thy field? from whence then hath it tares? He said unto them, An enemy hath done this. The servants said unto him, Wilt thou then that we go and gather them up? But he said, Nay; lest while ye gather up the tares, ye root up also the wheat with them. Let both grow together until the harvest: and in the time of harvest I will say to the reapers, Gather ye together first the tares, and bind them in bundles to burn them: but gather the wheat into my barn." Matthew 13:24-30.

It is obvious therefore that the Creator did not create a single noxious plant, thorn, or thistle. After sin entered, poisonous plants sprang up. In the parable of the sower the question was asked of the Master, "Didst not thou sow good seed in thy field? How then hath it tares?" The master answered, *"An enemy hath done this."* All thorns, thistles, and poisonous plants are the result of the perversion and degeneration caused by Satan's government of sin. The curse, then, is the result of sin. When God pronounced the curse He was simply announcing the results of transgression. Yet it was the judgement of God, for He judged correctly that since Adam had sold out the world to Satan's government, He (God) could do no more than to allow or permit Satan's government of sin to take over because that was man's choice.

But Satan's government is the curse! Only God's government can give and maintain order, beauty, perfection and life. Therefore when God handed the world over to Satan's government, He knew that degeneracy, disorder, decay, evil and death would be the terrible results of Adam's choice. When God pronounced the curse He was simply declaring the inevitable consequences of sin, consequences which come **not** from God but from that terrible separation from Him which sin causes.

As we approach the end, the concentration or intensity of sin in the world is rapidly and progressively increasing to the critical end point of separation.

The Spirit of God, persistently rejected, is gradually but definitely being withdrawn from the world. This means that the effects of the curse will become more and more severe as we approach the end.

> "This know also, that in the last days perilous times shall come. For men shall be lovers of their own selves, covetous, boasters, proud, blasphemers, disobedient to parents, unthankful, unholy, Without natural affection, trucebreakers, false accusers, incontinent, fierce, despisers of those that are good, Traitors, heady, highminded, lovers of pleasures more than lovers of God; Having a form of godliness, but denying the power thereof: from such turn away. For of this sort are they which creep into houses, and lead captive silly women laden with sins, led away with divers lusts, Ever learning, and never able to come to the knowledge of the truth. Now as Jannes and Jambres withstood Moses, so do these also resist the truth: men of corrupt minds, reprobate concerning the faith. But they shall proceed no further: for their folly shall be manifest unto all men, as theirs also was." 2 Tim. 3:1-9.

> "The land shall be utterly emptied, and utterly spoiled: for the Lord hath spoken this word. The earth mourneth and fadeth away, the world languisheth and fadeth away, the haughty people of the earth do languish. The earth also is defiled under the inhabitants thereof; because they have transgressed the laws, changed the ordinance, broken the everlasting covenant. Therefore hath the curse devoured the earth, and they that dwell therein are desolate: therefore the inhabitants of the earth are burned, and few men left." Isa. 24:3-6.

Eleven

Wars In The Old Testament

Another matter which perplexes many a thinking mind is the matter of warfare in the Old Testament. Why did God command the Israelites in Old Testament times to war and to kill? And if God is a God of war, how do we square that with the command to love our enemies?

The problem is not as difficult as it seems. All we need to do is to apply the interpretive Biblical principles mentioned in the past ten chapters.

First of all, let us go to Jesus. He is the One who declares the Father, who reveals the truth about God.

> *"For the law was given by Moses, but grace and truth came by Jesus Christ. No man hath seen God at any time; the only begotten Son, which is in the bosom of the Father, he hath declared him." John 1:17,18.*

> *"For God, who commanded the light to shine out of darkness, hath shined in our hearts, to give the light of the knowledge of the glory of God in the face of Jesus Christ."2 Cor. 4:6.*

What does Jesus teach about war and fighting? We turn to two gospel passages, John 18:36 and Matthew 26:51, 52.

> *"Jesus answered, My kingdom is not of this world: if my kingdom were of this world, then would my servants fight, that I should not be delivered to the Jews: but now is my kingdom not from hence." John 18:36*

> *"And, behold, one of them which were with Jesus stretched out his hand, and drew his sword, and struck a servant of the high priest's, and smote*

off his ear. Then said Jesus unto him, Put up again thy sword into his place: for all they that take the sword shall perish with the sword." Matthew 26:51, 52.

These passages of scripture clearly teach that neither fighting nor the use of coercive weapons of destruction has any place in the kingdom of God.

Wars and fights are the result of hatred, covetousness and illicit desire. In fact the self-centred or carnal mind is at war with God; is enmity against God and therefore at war with its fellowman as well.

"Then when lust hath conceived, it bringeth forth sin: and sin, when it is finished, bringeth forth death." James 1:15

"Ye adulterers and adulteresses, know ye not that the friendship of the world is enmity with God? whosoever therefore will be a friend of the world is the enemy of God." James 4:4

"For to be carnally minded is death; but to be spiritually minded is life and peace... So then they that are in the flesh cannot please God." Romans 8:6,8.

Therefore man's method of warfare is not God's method.

Many of the directives God gave to His ancient people were given because of the hardness of their hearts. When they stubbornly chose a way other than His way, God in His graciousness and love would give them the best advice on how to operate in the way which they chose. Meanwhile He would be patiently working to bring them back to His ideal way. But in most cases He was so misunderstood that the people believed their (wrong) way to be His or the ideal way!

Let us prove this from the Bible by listening to Jesus Himself, the True and Faithful Witness.

"The Pharisees also came unto him, tempting him, and saying unto him, Is it lawful for a man to put away his wife for every cause? And he answered and said unto them, Have ye not read, that he which made them at the beginning made them male and female, And said, For this cause shall a man leave father and mother, and shall cleave to his wife: and they twain shall be one flesh? Wherefore they are no more twain, but one flesh. What therefore God hath joined together, let not man put asunder. They say unto him, Why did Moses then command to give a writing of divorcement, and to put her away? He saith unto them, Moses because of the hardness of your hearts suffered you to put away your wives: but

from the beginning it was not so. And I say unto you, Whosoever shall put away his wife, except it be for fornication, and shall marry another, committeth adultery: and whoso marrieth her which is put away doth commit adultery." Matt. 19:3-9.

Jesus explained God's way for marriage. He then explained that hard-heartedness had led them to mistreat and put away their wives for any cause and, because of that, God through Moses had given advice on how best the putting away was to be done.

But "putting-away" or divorce is **not** God's way and therefore we are **not** to conclude that a particular command or directive is God's way without carefully studying the principles and circumstances involved.

So it was with polygamy and slavery. No Christian believes that either of these was or is God's will for mankind. God's ancient people copied these practices from the surrounding nations but God still continued to work along with them and even to give them advice on how best to administer or manage those particular ungodly traditions. (Read Lev. 25:39-55; Exodus 21:1-11).

We have already established from Jesus that military warfare is not of God, and therefore could not have been God's will for His ancient people. We can also prove this from the Old Testament. God delivered the Israelites from Egyptian bondage without their having to resort to warfare. His will for them was a warless march to the Promised Land. In fact He did not even want them to see war. Listen to the word of God in Exodus 13:17.

"And it came to pass, when Pharaoh had let the people go, that God led them not through the way of the land of the Philistines, although that was near; for God said, Lest peradventure the people repent when they see war, and they return to Egypt:" Exodus 13:17.

It was God's intention that just as He had delivered them from Egypt without their having to engage in military warfare, so too, He would deliver them from their enemies en route to the Promised Land. And this He told them in Deuteronomy 1:30.

"The Lord your God which goeth before you, he shall fight for you, according to all that he did for you in Egypt before your eyes;" Deut. 1:30.

We can correctly conclude therefore that it was not God's will for them to gain the Promised Land by warfare but by faith, which would produce strict obedience to all His laws.

But the Israelites departed gradually and progressively from God's way, choosing rather the way of military warfare. They also chose the way of civil punishments which their surrounding nations practiced. Eventually they chose the monarchial system for they wanted a king like all the other nations around them.

> *"Then all the elders of Israel gathered themselves together, and came to Samuel unto Ramah, And said unto him, Behold, thou art old, and thy sons walk not in thy ways: now make us a king to judge us like all the nations." 1 Sam. 8:4,5.*

By choosing a human king they were in fact rejecting God as their king.

> *"But the thing displeased Samuel, when they said, Give us a king to judge us. And Samuel prayed unto the Lord. And the Lord said unto Samuel, Hearken unto the voice of the people in all that they say unto thee: for they have not rejected thee, but they have rejected me, that I should not reign over them. According to all the works which they have done since the day that I brought them up out of Egypt even unto this day, wherewith they have forsaken me, and served other gods, so do they also unto thee." 1 Sam 8:6-8.*

God warned them of the results of the monarchial system.

> *"Now therefore hearken unto their voice: howbeit yet protest solemnly unto them, and shew them the manner of the king that shall reign over them. And Samuel told all the words of the Lord unto the people that asked of him a king. And he said, This will be the manner of the king that shall reign over you: He will take your sons, and appoint them for himself, for his chariots, and to be his horsemen; and some shall run before his chariots. And he will appoint him captains over thousands, and captains over fifties; and will set them to ear his ground, and to reap his harvest, and to make his instruments of war, and instruments of his chariots. And he will take your daughters to be confectionaries, and to be cooks, and to be bakers. And he will take your fields, and your vineyards, and your oliveyards, even the best of them, and give them to his servants. And he will take the tenth of your seed, and of your vineyards, and give to his officers, and to his servants. And he will take your menservants, and your maidservants, and your goodliest young men, and your asses, and put them to his work. He will take the tenth of your sheep: and ye shall*

be his servants. And ye shall cry out in that day because of your king which ye shall have chosen you; and the Lord will not hear you in that day." 1 Sam. 8:9-18.

Notwithstanding all this, the Israelites stubbornly persisted in demanding that they must have a king.

"Nevertheless the people refused to obey the voice of Samuel; and they said, Nay; but we will have a king over us; That we also may be like all the nations; and that our king may judge us, and go out before us, and fight our battles." 1Sam. 8: 19-20.

Pay careful attention to the three reasons they gave for wanting a king:
- to be like all the nations
- that the king may judge them
- that the king should go out before them and fight their battles

They therefore confirmed their choice of a judicial system and a military system like those of all the surrounding nations.

What God did next was an amazing revelation of His gracious character. Rather than rejecting them altogether, He offered to give them the best counsel in their worse choice.

God actually "selected" and anointed Israel's first king!

"And when Samuel saw Saul, the Lord said unto him, Behold the man whom I spake to thee of! this same shall reign over my people." 1 Sam. 9:17

"Then Samuel took a vial of oil, and poured it upon his head, and kissed him, and said, Is it not because the Lord hath anointed thee to be captain over his inheritance?... And Samuel said to all the people, See ye him whom the Lord hath chosen, that there is none like him among all the people? And all the people shouted, and said, God save the king." 1 Sam 10: 1, 24.

Anybody who reads 1 Samuel 10:1-24 without reading 1 Samuel 8 could and most likely would conclude that it was God's will for Israel to have a king.

But no, it was not. He was simply giving them the best advice and doing the most He could do for them in the wrong course they had chosen.

In the same way, since they had chosen the method of military warfare, all that God could do was to give them the best advice on how to operate within the wrong course they had already chosen.

In advising the Israelites about warfare God would indicate whether their enemy had "filled up the cup of their iniquity" that is, whether they had irreversibly cut themselves off from His righteousness.

If God had been doing it His way He would have "given up" the enemy to reap the full consequences of their iniquity and they would have met with total destruction without any military intervention by the Israelites. But since Israel had chosen their own monarchial, judicial and military systems, all that God could do was to give them the best counsel under the prevailing circumstances. He commanded Israel to utterly wipe out the enemy by their chosen military method. But just as how His command to Samuel to choose and to anoint a king is not to be interpreted to mean that the monarchial system is God's way, neither are we to interpret His military commands to mean that the way of military warfare is God's way.

There is an interesting account in 1Samuel 15 which is worth reading.

Why did God command Saul to kill all the Amalekites?

Israel had chosen the monarchial and military system and therefore God could not use Hs method in their behalf, this they had rejected.

The Amalekites had passed their limit in sin; they were irreversibly set against God. If God were employing His way He would have "withdrawn" from the Amalekites and they would have perished.

If Saul had brought back any Amalekite property to Israel he would have brought into the Camp of Israel that which had been separated from God and would have put Israel at risk of forfeiting the Divine protection. Thus the best advice God could have given was the one He had given.

We have already seen that Jesus (in Matthew 5) explained the difference between directives given to the people because of their stubbornness in following the way of the world on one hand and on the other, God's ideal will.

Here is another example.

> "Ye have heard that it hath been said, An eye for an eye, and a tooth for a tooth: But I say unto you, That ye resist not evil: but whosoever shall smite thee on thy right cheek, turn to him the other also." Matt. 5:38,39.

What a wonderful God. He worked along with His people in their wrong ways while always seeking to lead them to His perfect ways.

Twelve

The Language Problem

Again we start this chapter by going back to the text which holds the key to correct interpretation of the scriptures.

> *"For what man knoweth the things of a man, save the spirit of man which is in him? even so the things of God knoweth no man, but the Spirit of God. Now we have received, not the spirit of the world, but the spirit which is of God; that we might know the things that are freely given to us of God.*
>
> *Which things also we speak, not in the words which man's wisdom teacheth, but which the Holy Ghost teacheth; comparing spiritual things with spiritual. But the natural man receiveth not the things of the Spirit of God: for they are foolishness unto him: neither can he know them, because they are spiritually discerned." 1 Cor. 2:11-14.*

The natural mind cannot receive the deep eternal truths of the Divine Nature and character. In fact, the real truth of God's character and ways is foolishness to the natural mind!

We need the Holy Spirit in order to understand the deep things of God. The Spirit of God in the word of God enables the spiritually-minded searcher for truth to arrive at truth by comparing spiritual things with spiritual. This means allowing scripture to interpret scripture.

God's ways and thoughts are infinitely higher than our human ways and thoughts. Moreover, the Bible is written in human language which is imperfect. Therefore we must allow God to tell us what He means when the Bible uses certain human words to describe His ways. God must give us the true understanding of His word.

"For my thoughts are not your thoughts, neither are your ways my ways, saith the Lord. For as the heavens are higher than the earth, so are my ways higher than your ways, and my thoughts than your thoughts." Isaiah 55:8,9

"And we know that the Son of God is come, and hath given us an understanding, that we may know him that is true, and we are in him that is true, even in his Son Jesus Christ. This is the true God, and eternal life." 1 John 5:20.

There is one very critically important principle which must be understood in order to correctly interpret statements about God's behaviour. It is this:

The bible describes God as doing that which he permits or that which he does not prevent.

Let us prove this principle from the Bible. Read 1 Chronicles 10: 13-14:

"So Saul died for his transgression which he committed against the Lord, even against the word of the Lord, which he kept not, and also for asking counsel of one that had a familiar spirit, to enquire of it; And enquired not of the Lord: therefore he slew him, and turned the kingdom unto David the son of Jesse." 1 Chron. 10:13-14.

Verse 14 clearly states that God slew king Saul. Now read how Saul was actually killed in the earlier verses of the same chapter, 1 Chronicles chapter 10:

"And the battle went sore against Saul, and the archers hit him, and he was wounded of the archers. Then said Saul to his armourbearer, Draw thy sword, and thrust me through therewith; lest these uncircumcised come and abuse me. But his armourbearer would not; for he was sore afraid. So Saul took a sword, and fell upon it. And when his armourbearer saw that Saul was dead, he fell likewise on the sword, and died. So Saul died, and his three sons, and all his house died together." 1 Chron. 10: 3-6.

King Saul had turned away from God very early in his career as king. He had stubbornly rebelled against the command of God concerning the war with the Amalekites. Listen to what Samuel had told him in 1 Samuel 15: 23.

"For rebellion is as the sin of witchcraft, and stubbornness is as iniquity and idolatry. Because thou hast rejected the word of the Lord, he hath also rejected thee from being king." 1 Sam. 15:23.

Saul, having separated himself from God by his own iniquity, went to war without God's protection. God "gave him up" and "permitted" his enemies to kill him.

Bible language says, "God slew him", but that means he was separated from God's protection and God could have done nothing to help him. What God permitted, He is described as doing. Let us now consider another example:

> *"And again the anger of the Lord was kindled against Israel, and he moved David against them to say, Go, number Israel and Judah." 2 Sam. 24:1.*

Here again the text plainly states that God moved (or tempted) David to number Israel and Judah. But to number Israel was to commit sin because God had previously commanded that such was not to be done. In fact David's conscience pricked him after he had numbered Israel.

> *"And David's heart smote him after that he had numbered the people. And David said unto the Lord, I have sinned greatly in that I have done: and now, I beseech thee, O Lord, take away the iniquity of thy servant; for I have done very foolishly." 2 Sam. 24:10.*

How could God have moved David to commit sin when, according to James 1:13, God does not tempt or move anyone to sin?

> *"Let no man say when he is tempted, I am tempted of God: for God cannot be tempted with evil, neither tempteth he any man:" James 1:13.*

Obviously what 2 Samuel 24:1 is really saying is that God permitted David to be moved or tempted by Satan. God has given us all freedom of choice, we can choose to give in to sinful desires or we can choose to resist such desires by God's enabling grace.

This interpretation of 2 Samuel 24:1 is confirmed in 1 Chronicles 21:1 which describes exactly the same event but informs us that it was Satan who moved David to sin by numbering Israel!

> *"And Satan stood up against Israel, and provoked David to number Israel." 1 Chron. 21:1.*

For example number 3 we turn to Isaiah 45:7 and Amos 3:6.

> *"I form the light, and create darkness: I make peace, and create evil: I the Lord do all these things." Isaiah 45:7*

> *"Shall a trumpet be blown in the city, and the people not be afraid? shall there be evil in a city, and the Lord hath not done it?" Amos 3:6*

These passages declare that God creates evil, that God does evil. But what is the correct interpretation and understanding of such statements? First of all let us prove that God is **never** the source of evil that He **never** does evil.

"Thou are of purer eyes than to behold evil, and canst not look on iniquity: wherefore lookest thou upon them that deal treacherously, and holdest thy tongue when the wicked devoureth the man that is more righteous than he?" Hab. 1:13.

"The Lord is righteous in all his ways, and holy in all his works." Psalm 145:17

"He that committeth sin is of the devil; for the devil sinneth from the beginning. For this purpose the Son of God was manifested, that he might destroythe works of the devil. Whosoever is born of God doth not commit sin; for his seed remaineth in him: and he cannot sin, because he is born of God. In this the children of God are manifest, and the children of the devil: whosoever doeth not righteousness is not of God, neither he that loveth not his brother." 1 John 3:8-10

"Let no man say when he is tempted, I am tempted of God: for God cannot be tempted with evil, neither tempteth he any man: But every man is tempted, when he is drawn away of his own lust, and enticed. Then when lust hath conceived, it bringeth forth sin: and sin, when it is finished, bringeth forth death. Do not err, my beloved brethren. Every good gift and every perfect gift is from above, and cometh down from the Father of lights, with whom is no variableness, neither shadow of turning." James 1:13-17

These passages of scripture teach, incontrovertibly, that God is never the cause nor the source of evil. Therefore when passages like Isaiah 45:7 and Amos 3:6 state that God creates evil or does evil, the only correct interpretation must be that God allows or permits evil.

Satan's government of sin is the source and cause of all evil. God is the Source of all good. This is further confirmed by Job. 2:10.

"But he said unto her, Thou speakest as one of the foolish women speaketh. What? shall we receive good at the hand of God, and shall we not receive evil? In all this did not Job sin with his lips." Job 2:10.

How did Job receive evil at the hand of God? He received evil at the hand of God when God permitted Satan to strike him with evil.

Darkness is symbolic of sin and all its evil consequences. Light is symbolic of righteousness and all its results of **good**. Listen again to the message which Jesus brought to earth about His Father.

> *"This then is the message which we have heard of him, and declare unto you, that God is light, and in him is no darkness at all." 1 John 1:5.*

This brings us to another critically important principle of correct interpretation of statements concerning God's behaviour. It is this:

Whenever any passage of scripture describes God as causing or doing evil, it must be interpreted to mean that he permits or allows the evil to be done by the agencies of Satan and sin.

God does not do evil, in fact He cannot do evil.

> *"Let love be without dissimulation. Abhor that which is evil; cleave to that which is good... Be not overcome of evil, but overcome evil with good." Romans 12:9, 21*

> *"But unto the Son he saith, Thy throne, O God, is for ever and ever: a sceptre of righteousness is the sceptre of thy kingdom. Thou hast loved righteousness, and hated iniquity; therefore God, even thy God, hath anointed thee with the oil of gladness above thy fellows." Hebrews 1:8, 9.*

There are many recorded cases of punishments inflicted upon Israel in the Old Testament. These punishments are often described as being inflicted by God's direct decree or direct action. The problem is that most people go no deeper than the apparent meaning of the words and therefore believe that God rather than sin, was the source or cause of the calamities and destructions which befell ancient Israel. In fact the Israelites were but reaping the consequences of their own sins when God withdrew from them and permitted the forces of evil to strike them.

> *"Is Israel a servant? is he a homeborn slave? why is he spoiled? The young lions roared upon him, and yelled, and they made his land waste: his cities are burned without inhabitant. Also the children of Noph and Tahapanes have broken the crown of thy head. Hast thou not procured this unto thyself, in that thou hast forsaken the Lord thy God, when he led thee by the way? And now what hast thou to do in the way of Egypt, to drink the waters of Sihor? or what hast thou to do in the way of Assyria, to drink the waters of the river? Thine own wickedness shall correct thee,*

and thy backslidings shall reprove thee: know therefore and see that it is an evil thing and bitter, that thou hast forsaken the Lord thy God, and that my fear is not in thee, saith the Lord God of hosts." Jer. 2:14-19

"Thy way and thy doings have procured these things unto thee; this is thy wickedness, because it is bitter, because it reacheth unto thine heart." Jer. 4:18

We can be sure of this because even before the punishments were inflicted on the Israelites God forewarned them.

In Deuteronomy 28:15-28, Moses had given them a list of the punishments which would befall them if they persisted in disobedience. The language is the typical punitive language where God is described as saying:

> *"I will destroy thee, ….*
> *"I will smite thee….*
> *"I will send enemies ….*
> *"I will send pestilence… etc.*

But the correct way to interpret **all** these statements is given in Deuteronomy 31:16-18:

"And the Lord said unto Moses, Behold, thou shalt sleep with thy fathers; and this people will rise up, and go a whoring after the gods of the strangers of the land, whither they go to be among them, and will forsake me, and break my covenant which I have made with them. Then my anger shall be kindled against them in that day, and I will forsake them, and I will hide my face from them, and they shall be devoured, and many evils and troubles shall befall them; so that they will say in that day, Are not these evils come upon us, because our God is not among us? And I will surely hide my face in that day for all the evils which they shall have wrought, in that they are turned unto other gods." Deut. 31:16-18.

All their punishments, every single one, resulted when God withdrew from them because they rejected him, his love, his truth and his righteousness.

And since this is true in their case it must be true in all other instances of punishments anywhere, anytime, anyhow, because God cannot change and the principles of His dealing with men and sin are consistent and constant.

> *"For I am the Lord, I change not; therefore ye sons of Jacob are not consumed." Malachi 3:6*

> *"Every good gift and every perfect gift is from above, and cometh down from the Father of lights, with whom is no variableness, neither shadow of turning." James 1:17.*

The argument so often put forward, that **withdrawal** is but one method and there are other methods is utterly false because every description of God inflicting punishment because of sin has the same mechanism of **withdrawal by God**. For anyone to read any statement about God causing evil or doing evil or destroying or smiting or sending disaster, and interpret it as a direct act of God, is to completely reject the correct principles of interpretation which have been so clearly laid down in the word of God.

We can now look at seven other examples which will further confirm that our principles of linguistic interpretation are absolutely correct.

One:

> *"And the Lord said, Who shall persuade Ahab, that he may go up and fall at Ramothgilead? And one said on this manner, and another said on that manner. And there came forth a spirit, and stood before the Lord, and said, I will persuade him. And the Lord said unto him, Wherewith? And he said, I will go forth, and I will be a lying spirit in the mouth of all his prophets. And he said, Thou shalt persuade him, and prevail also: go forth, and do so. Now therefore, behold, the Lord hath put a lying spirit in the mouth of all these thy prophets, and the Lord hath spoken evil concerning thee." 1 Kings 22:20-23*

Verse 23 states that the Lord **put** a lying spirit in the mouth of the false prophets. But God cannot lie.

> *"That by two immutable things, in which it was impossible for God to lie, we might have a strong consolation, who have fled for refuge to lay hold upon the hope set before us:" Hebrews 6:18.*

> *"In hope of eternal life, which God, that cannot lie, promised before the world began;" Titus 1:2.*

Therefore there must be a **correct** way of understanding 1 Kings 22:23.

The prophets and the king chose to reject God's true warnings and to accept a message of false security. Since God permits freedom of choice, Bible language describes Him as **doing** what He **permits.** In reality God did not cause a lie to be told, rather He gave them up to believe the lies they wanted to hear.

Similarly in 2 Thess 2:11 it is written that "… God shall send them strong delusion that they should believe a lie." But God is not in the business of deceiving people or causing them to believe lies. In fact what happens is this, as men reject the truths of His word, God withdraws His Spirit and leaves them to the deceptions which they love.

> *"Even him, whose coming is after the working of Satan with all power and signs and lying wonders, And with all deceivableness of unrighteousness in them that perish; because they received not the love of the truth, that they might be saved. And for this cause God shall send them strong delusion, that they should believe a lie: That they all might be damned who believed not the truth, but had pleasure in unrighteousness." 2 Thess. 2: 9-12.*

Two — Who hardens hearts?

> *"And the Lord said unto Moses, When thou goest to return into Egypt, see that thou do all those wonders before Pharaoh, which I have put in thine hand: but I will harden his heart, that he shall not let the people go." Exodus 4:21.*

> *"For it was of the Lord to harden their hearts, that they should come against Israel in battle, that he might destroy them utterly, and that they might have no favour, but that he might destroy them, as the Lord commanded Moses." Joshua 11:20.*

These passages state that God hardened the heart of Pharaoh and the hearts of Israel's enemies.

Bible language describes God as **doing** what He **permits**. People have the freedom of choice to respond positively to God in voluntary submission to His will or to respond negatively by rejecting His will and resisting His Spirit.

In other words **people harden their own hearts by resisting God's Spirit and rejecting His love, His truth and His righteousness.** God **does not** harden any person's heart.

> *"But when Pharaoh saw that there was respite, he hardened his heart, and hearkened not unto them; as the Lord had said… And Pharaoh hardened his heart at this time also, neither would he let the people go." Exodus 8:15, 32*

> *"Wherefore as the Holy Ghost saith, To day if ye will hear his voice, Harden not your hearts, as in the provocation, in the day of temptation in the wilderness:" Hebrews 3:7,8.*

The Spirit of God persistently rejected is at last withdrawn, leaving the soul unimpressionable by truth and fixed in error.

Three:

> *"And the Lord sent fiery serpents among the people, and they bit the people; and much people of Israel died." Numbers 21:6.*

Here again notice the language. It says "God sent fiery serpents...." We said earlier how God sends strong delusion. He sends strong delusion by withdrawing His Spirit from those whose minds are fixed against His truth.

Similarly the statement "God **sent** fiery serpents" means God withdrew His protection and the fiery serpents attacked them because their sin of persistent murmuring and unbelief had separated them partially from God's protection.

Four:

> *"Awake, O sword, against my shepherd, and against the man that is my fellow, saith the Lord of hosts: smite the shepherd, and the sheep shall be scattered: and I will turn mine hand upon the little ones." Zechariah 13:7*

> *"And Jesus saith unto them, All ye shall be offended because of me this night: for it is written, I will smite the shepherd, and the sheep shall be scattered." Mark 14:27*

These passages state that Christ was **struck** and **smitten** by His Father. In actuality our sins, the sins of the entire world separated Him from His Father. His Father **spared Him not** but **delivered Him** up to the consequences of sin for us. This was the mechanism of Christ's death.

> *"For he hath made him to be sin for us, who knew no sin; that we might be made the righteousness of God in him." 2 Cor. 5:21.*

> *"And about the ninth hour Jesus cried with a loud voice, saying, Eli, Eli, lama sabachthani? that is to say, My God, my God, why hast thou forsaken me?" Matthew 27: 46.*

Five:

> "And Samuel came no more to see Saul until the day of his death: nevertheless Samuel mourned for Saul: and the Lord repented that He had made Saul king over Israel." 1Sam. 15:35

This text states that God **repented** that He had made Saul king over Israel. Similarly in Genesis 6:6 we are told that:

> "It repented the Lord that He had made man on the earth, and it grieved Him at His heart." Gen. 6:6.

But we are told elsewhere that:

> "God is not a man, that He should lie; neither the Son of man, that he should repent: hath He said, and shall he not do it? Or hath He spoken and shall He not make good?" Numbers 23:19.

Here again we are faced with the **language problem**, an apparent contradiction in scripture.

Since God knows the end from the beginning, since He foreknew all that would ever happen, He is never caught by surprise, He never does anything and then regrets doing it!

God, in His infinite love for all of us, wishes that we make a success of our most important work in life, the work of character building.

When any person follows a path of wickedness it hurts God's heart of love and the language which says *"God repented that he anointed Saul as King over Israel"* really means that God was deeply hurt by the course of disobedience which Saul followed. HE was similarly very hurt by the wicked life styles of the antediluvians, in fact Genesis 6:6 explains itself when it states that:

> "It repented the Lord that He had made man on the earth, and it grieved Him at His heart." Gen. 6:6.

Six:

> "For I will pass through the land of Egypt this night, and will smite all the firstborn in the land of Egypt, both man and beast; and against all the gods of Egypt I will execute judgment: I am the Lord. And the blood shall be to you for a token upon the houses where ye are: and when I see the blood, I will pass over you and the plague shall not be upon you to destroy you, when I smite the land of Egypt." Exodus 12:12,13

Notice the language here again but also notice the explanation in verse 23.

> *"For the Lord will pass through to smite the Egyptians; and when he seeth the blood upon the lintel, and on the two side posts, the Lord will pass over the door, and will not suffer the destroyer to come in unto your houses to smite you." Exodus12:23.*

God's protection prevented destruction. When the people were separated from that protection the destroyer smote the first born. Why was the first born more susceptible? The Egyptians dedicated their first born to their gods.

Seven — The Case of Korah:

The account of the divine judgement which befell Korah is written down in Numbers 16:28-35. The Apostle Paul gives a list of the divine judgments which occurred on the long journey toward the Promised Land. No one is left out. Here it is.

> *"Do not become idolaters as were some of them (Exodus 32). Nor let us commit sexual immorality, as some of them did, and in one day twenty-three thousand fell (Numbers 25:1-9); nor let us tempt Christ, as some of them also tempted, and were destroyed by serpents (Numbers 2:6-9); nor murmur, as some of them also murmured, and were destroyed by the destroyer."*

And we know who he is. The destroyer is Satan and his government of sin (John 10:10; Job. 1:12).

The last entry of complainers, destroyed by the destroyer, includes the quail eaters (Exodus 16; Numbers 11), the Kadesh-Barnea rebels (Numbers 13,14; Deuteronomy 1:19-46; 2:14-16); and Korah, Dathan and Abiram (Numbers 16, 17).

We close this chapter by restating the two fundamental principles of biblical linguistic interpretation concerning passages which describe God's actions or behaviour.

> ***The bible describes God as doing what he allows or permits or what he does not prevent.***

> ***Whenever any passage of scripture describes god as causing, doing, or sending evil or calamity, it must be interpreted to mean that he allows or permits the evil by withdrawing his protection and restraint.***

Thirteen

God Protects

It was Election Day in the Garden of Eden. The instructions were clear. Adam, as the Representative Man for all humanity, had freedom of choice. If he obeyed God he would be choosing God's government to **continue** its perfect maintenance of a perfect world. On the other hand, if he disobeyed God he would be **rejecting** God's government and **choosing** Satan's government of sin to take over the running of affairs on our planet.

God had made a perfect world. Adam and Eve were perfect in structure and function and innocent in character. (Read Genesis chapters 1-3)

Satan planned his campaign strategy with masterful cunning and well calculated deception. He would approach Adam through Eve, after approaching her through what was then, the most beautiful of creatures, the serpent.

The word of God was clear and unequivocal. *"Thou shalt not eat of the fruit of the tree of the knowledge of good and evil, disobedience will result in death."*

Satan told his first lie on earth when he told Eve *"you will not die if you disobey God."* Gen. 3.4,5.

Eve disobeyed God and then Satan used her to get to Adam's mind. Adam also disobeyed. Adam's disobedience sold out our world to Satan's government of sin and separated our world from the perfect maintenance which only God's government can give. Paul summarises these facts in one succinct statement in Romans 5:12.

> *"Wherefore, as by one man sin entered into the world, and death by sin; and so death passed upon all men, for that all have sinned:"* *Romans 5:12.*

The wonderful powers of creation, the wonderful mechanisms and systems of nature, the geophysical and biological powers which had all been created perfectly were now separated from God's perfect government.

These created powers and systems became spoiled, deranged and disordered. **They became perverted** and inherently self-destructive, and as time passed their malfunction became more heavily felt by man and beast and planet.

But God and His Son were not caught off guard by the entrance of sin into our world. The Plan of Redemption, devised from all eternity past, was immediately put into operation. The Son of God became the surety for the lost race and God immediately put into effect His protective and remedial government of grace to hold in check the sin-spoiled powers of biology, physics, chemistry and geography on our planet and also on its relevant and necessary surroundings in outer space.

The Spirit of God, working through the angels of God, holds in check and restrains the perverted powers of a fallen creation of our planet. If God were to **let go** or **withdraw** this restraint the perverted powers of nature would malfunction so severely that it would be impossible for human life to survive on earth.

> *"It is of the Lord 's mercies that we are not consumed, because his compassions fail not. They are new every morning: great is thy faithfulness." Lam. 3:22,23*

> *"The thief cometh not, but for to steal, and to kill, and to destroy: I am come that they might have life, and that they might have it more abundantly." John 10:10*

> *"Let no man say when he is tempted, I am tempted of God: for God cannot be tempted with evil, neither tempteth he any man: But every man is tempted, when he is drawn away of his own lust, and enticed. Then when lust hath conceived, it bringeth forth sin: and sin, when it is finished, bringeth forth death. Do not err, my beloved brethren. Every good gift and every perfect gift is from above, and cometh down from the Father of lights, with whom is no variableness, neither shadow of turning." James 1:13-17*

The function of the angels to hold in check the forces of evil is described in Revelation 7:1.

"And after these things I saw four angels standing on the four corners of the earth, holding the four winds of the earth, that the wind should not blow on the earth, nor on the sea, nor on any tree." Rev. 7:1.

In Jeremiah 25:32 we are told that the "winds of the earth" symbolize the forces of evil and we are also given a description of what happens when these "winds" or forces of evil are let go.

"A noise shall come even to the ends of the earth; for the Lord hath a controversy with the nations, he will plead with all flesh; he will give them that are wicked to the sword, saith the Lord. Thus saith the Lord of hosts, Behold, evil shall go forth from nation to nation, and a great whirlwind shall be raised up from the coasts of the earth. And the slain of the Lord shall be at that day from one end of the earth even unto the other end of the earth: they shall not be lamented, neither gathered, nor buried; they shall be dung upon the ground." Jeremiah 25:31-33.

We must always remember that destruction never comes because of any **change** in God, it is the result of people **forsaking** God and therefore **rejecting** His **protection**.

"For I am the Lord, I change not; therefore ye sons of Jacob are not consumed." Malachi 3:6

"And the Spirit of God came upon Azariah the son of Oded: And he went out to meet Asa, and said unto him, Hear ye me, Asa, and all Judah and Benjamin; The Lord is with you, while ye be with him; and if ye seek him, he will be found of you; but if ye forsake him, he will forsake you." 2 Chron. 15: 1,2

"O Lord, the hope of Israel, all that forsake thee shall be ashamed, and they that depart from me shall be written in the earth, because they have forsaken the Lord, the fountain of living waters." Jeremiah 17:13

"Behold, the Lord's hand is not shortened, that it cannot save; neither his ear heavy, that it cannot hear: But your iniquities have separated between you and your God, and your sins have hid his face from you, that he will not hear." Isaiah 59:1,2.

We have already studied the story of Job. We saw that Satan knows that God graciously supplies a hedge of protection.

"Then Satan answered the Lord, and said, Doth Job fear God for nought? Hast not thou made an hedge about him, and about his house, and about all that he hath on every side? thou hast blessed the work of his hands, and his substance is increased in the land." Job 1:9,10.

When the hedge was withdrawn the "winds" of strife, which were kept under restraint, not only collapsed into malfunction but were further manipulated by Satan into "whirlwinds" of destruction.

God is the Protector. Satan, with his government of sin, is the destroyer. It is only by the mercies of God that we are able to survive at all.

While it is true that the whole world enjoys general protection (Revelation 7:1) we must also understand that those who believe in God and are surrendered to His will through faith in Jesus Christ enjoy special protection like Job did.

"The angel of the Lord encampeth round about them that fear him, and delivereth them." Psalm 34:7.

"Then said Daniel unto the king, O king, live for ever. My God hath sent his angel, and hath shut the lions' mouths, that they have not hurt me: forasmuch as before him innocency was found in me; and also before thee, O king, have I done no hurt." Daniel 6:21, 22.

When Christians understand these important truths and give praise to God with thanksgiving, they actually allow the Holy Spirit to tighten the protective hedge about them and thereby render Satan's attacks ineffective! (For private study read all of 2 Chronicles chapter 20; notice verses 21, 22).

We can also look again at Deuteronomy chapter 28, the chapter of blessings and curses. When God's protective hedge was tightened around Israel the forces of nature were kept in functional order, but when they forsook God and forfeited His protection the forces of nature malfunctioned with severely disastrous consequences upon their shelterless heads.

All of this teaches us how malignant sin is and why God, through the plan of salvation in Jesus Christ, has given to us everything we need to be completely cleansed of all sin and be totally filled with His righteousness. Complete victory over sin is an absolute necessity and is guaranteed in Jesus Christ. Remember that sin is spiritual cancer and whatever defects we do not overcome will overcome us and work out our utter ruin in the end.

Making Up The Hedge

Genuine born-again believers have a very important and critical work to do in maintaining the functional integrity of the **protective hedge**.

> *"And I sought for a man among them, that should make up the hedge, and stand in the gap before me for the land, that I should not destroy it: but I found none. Therefore have I poured out mine indignation upon them; I have consumed them with the fire of my wrath: their own way have I recompensed upon their heads, saith the Lord God." Ezekiel 22:30-31.*

By persistent, insistent, consistent, heart-felt, earnest, intercessory conversational prayer, the people of God will move the Arm of Omnipotence to strengthen the angelic hedge of protection and to intensify the work of the Holy Spirit in the saving of souls.

When we understand how wonderfully good God is, when we understand the truth about His lovely character, our prayers will take the form of a conversation with Him and His Son. In fact when we know God aright, as is our privilege, our trust in Him, our love for Him and our prayer-lives will all be deepened and enriched. Our prayers will be prayers of strong faith which will bring definite and certain answer to our petitions.

> *"If my people, which are called by my name, shall humble themselves, and pray, and seek my face, and turn from their wicked ways; then will I hear from heaven, and will forgive their sin, and will heal their land." 2 Chron. 7:14.*

> *"Is any among you afflicted? let him pray. Is any merry? let him sing psalms. Is any sick among you? let him call for the elders of the church; and let them pray over him, anointing him with oil in the name of the Lord: And the prayer of faith shall save the sick, and the Lord shall raise him up; and if he have committed sins, they shall be forgiven him. Confess your faults one to another, and pray one for another, that ye may be healed. The effectual fervent prayer of a righteous man availeth much." James 5:13-16.*

> *"Pray without ceasing. In every thing give thanks: for this is the will of God in Christ Jesus concerning you." 1 Thess. 5:17,18.*

Fourteen

Not By Might Nor By Power

Because we live in this sinful world, we have become so well educated in the ways of Satan's government to such an extent that it is very difficult for us to understand that there are other ways, indeed better ways, of doing things.

We have grown all too accustomed to the routine of sinful living in a sinful world where the use of force is commonplace. In order to overcome criminals and evil men the law-enforcing agencies must use superior force and fighting power to crush out the criminal element. Sinful man has no other way.

God has even given to our sinful world the good advice, in fact the best advice, on how to deal with the unruly:

> *"Let every soul be subject unto the higher powers. For there is no power but of God: the powers that be are ordained of God. Whosoever therefore resisteth the power, resisteth the ordinance of God: and they that resist shall receive to themselves damnation. For rulers are not a terror to good works, but to the evil. Wilt thou then not be afraid of the power? do that which is good, and thou shalt have praise of the same: For he is the minister of God to thee for good. But if thou do that which is evil, be afraid; for he beareth not the sword in vain: for he is the minister of God, a revenger to execute wrath upon him that doeth evil. Wherefore ye must needs be subject, not only for wrath, but also for conscience sake. For for this cause pay ye tribute also: for they are God's ministers, attending continually upon this very thing. Render therefore to all their dues: tribute to whom tribute is due; custom to whom custom; fear to whom fear; honour to whom honour." Romans 13:1-7.*

You will remember that God appointed Israel a king when they chose to be like all the other nations. Similarly, God has permitted and appointed the judicial system, magistrates and judges and the court system to allow those accused to be given a fair trial and, if found guilty, to be given the appropriate punishment. He permitted ancient Israel to use the death penalty for severe civil or criminal offences.

In a sinful world where the vast majority care nothing for God's ways there must be a method of dealing with those whose behaviour threaten the stability, order and livelihood of society. That method is the civil-criminal-justice system with the judiciary and fair court trials which make decisions and execute just punishments based on the rule of law and the equality of all men before the law.

But all of this is still the way of the world. It is the best of all the systems of worldly justice, but it is still the way of the world.

- What is God's perfect way for dealing with His enemies?
- Does God use force to put down rebellion?
- Does God crush His enemies, killing them by violent, coercive destructive force?
- Is God the executioner of sinners?
- Will God overcome Satan's government of sin by the power of might or by the power of right?

These are questions which must be answered honestly and truthfully. Let us, in fact, begin with Zechariah 4:6.

> *"Then he answered and spake unto me, saying, This is the word of the Lord unto Zerubbabel, saying, Not by might, nor by power, but by my spirit, saith the Lord of hosts." Zechariah 4:6.*

However massive the problem, God solves it not by might nor by power but by His Spirit.

God is love. His nature, His law is love. The very essence of God's Spirit is Agapé love, which is an **all-for-the-other** love.

> *"He that loveth not knoweth not God; for God is love." 1 John 4:8, 16.*

> *"Love worketh no ill to his neighbour: therefore love is the fulfilling of the law." Romans 13:10.*

The principle of unselfish, self-sacrificing ever-giving love is the foundation of God's Government. It is a principle from which God never varies even to the slightest degree. It is a principle from which He can never change.

"For I am the Lord, I change not; therefore ye sons of Jacob are not consumed." Malachi 3:6.

"Every good gift and every perfect gift is from above, and cometh down from the Father of lights, with whom is no variableness, neither shadow of turning." James 1:17.

The infinite, eternal, selfless, Agapé love of God is functionally constituted in the Holy Spirit.

"And hope maketh not ashamed; because the love of God is shed abroad in our hearts by the Holy Ghost which is given unto us." Romans 5:5.

So we can go back to Zechariah 4:6 and understand what God is saying to us:

Not by might nor by power but by my spirit of infinite love.

Not by force but by love, not by might but by right, this is God's perfect way, this is the method by which He triumphs over those who oppose His Government. And this is the method by which He will ultimately triumph over Satan's government of sin.

"Love suffereth long, and is kind; Love envieth not; love vaunteth not itself, is not puffed up, Doth not behave itself unseemly, seeketh not her own, is not easily provoked, thinketh no evil; Rejoiceth not in iniquity, but rejoiceth in the truth; Beareth all things, believeth all things, hopeth all things, endureth all things. Love never faileth: but whether there be prophecies, they shall fail; whether there be tongues, they shall cease; whether there be knowledge, it shall vanish away." 1 Cor. 13:4-8

"For we can do nothing against the truth, but for the truth." 2 Cor. 13:8.

How Does God Treat His Enemies?

In The Sermon on the Mount, Jesus gave to the world the correct understanding of the foundation principles of God's government. In fact, He contrasted the way of the world with the way of God's kingdom.

"But I say unto you which hear, Love your enemies, do good to them which hate you, Bless them that curse you, and pray for them which despitefully use you. And unto him that smiteth thee on the one cheek offer also the other; and him that taketh away thy cloke forbid not to take thy coat also. Give to every man that asketh of thee; and of him that taketh away thy goods ask them not again. And as ye would that men should do to you, do

ye also to them likewise. For if ye love them which love you, what thank have ye? for sinners also love those that love them. And if ye do good to them which do good to you, what thank have ye? for sinners also do even the same. And if ye lend to them of whom ye hope to receive, what thank have ye? for sinners also lend to sinners, to receive as much again. But love ye your enemies, and do good, and lend, hoping for nothing again; and your reward shall be great, and ye shall be the children of the Highest: for he is kind unto the unthankful and to the evil. Be ye therefore merciful, as your Father also is merciful." Luke 6:27-36.

God loves His enemies and does only good to them. God is changeless. He is the giver only of good gifts. His love for His creatures is always unconditional and with Him there is not the slightest tendency of variation. He constantly and consistently does only good to all because that is His nature.

"Every good gift and every perfect gift is from above, and cometh down from the Father of lights, with whom is no variableness, neither shadow of turning." James 1:17

"The Lord is righteous in all his ways, and holy in all his works." Psalm 145:17.

"In the way of righteousness is life; and in the pathway thereof there is no death." Proverbs 12:28.

How Does God Overcome Evil?

"Be not overcome of evil, but overcome evil with good." Romans 12:21.

God's way is the way of overcoming evil with good. He does not retaliate. He does not return evil for evil.

"For even hereunto were ye called: because Christ also suffered for us, leaving us an example, that ye should follow his steps: Who did no sin, neither was guile found in his mouth: Who, when he was reviled, reviled not again; when he suffered, he threatened not; but committed himself to him that judgeth righteously:" 1 Peter 2:21-23.

"Or despisest thou the riches of his goodness and forbearance and longsuffering; not knowing that the goodness of God leadeth thee to repentance?" Romans 2:4.

How Then Are His Enemies Destroyed?

God loves everyone. In fact it was when we were still His enemies that He demonstrated His unconditional love for us by sending His Son to die to reconcile us to Himself.

> *"For when we were yet without strength, in due time Christ died for the ungodly. For scarcely for a righteous man will one die: yet peradventure for a good man some would even dare to die. But God commendeth his love toward us, in that, while we were yet sinners, Christ died for us."*
> *Romans 5:6-8.*

> *"For ye know the grace of our Lord Jesus Christ, that, though he was rich, yet for your sakes he became poor, that ye through his poverty might be rich." 2 Cor. 8:9.*

Those who respond positively to His love are saved from sin and its wages. But those who persistently and irreversibly reject God's love eventually cut themselves off from God Who is the Source of Life, and suffer destruction including, ultimately, the second death.

> *"For whoso findeth me findeth life, and shall obtain favour of the LORD. But he that sinneth against me wrongeth his own soul: all they that hate me love death." Proverbs 8:35, 36.*

> *"And this is the record, that God hath given to us eternal life, and this life is in his Son. He that hath the Son hath life; and he that hath not the Son of God hath not life." 1 John 5:11,12*

> *"O Lord, the hope of Israel, all that forsake thee shall be ashamed, and they that depart from me shall be written in the earth, because they have forsaken the Lord, the fountain of living waters." Jeremiah 17:13.*

> *"Thine own wickedness shall correct thee, and thy backslidings shall reprove thee: know therefore and see that it is an evil thing and bitter, that thou hast forsaken the Lord thy God, and that my fear is not in thee, saith the Lord God of hosts.*

> *"For my people have committed two evils; they have forsaken me the fountain of living waters, and hewed them out cisterns, broken cisterns, that can hold no water." Jeremiah 2:19, 13.*

> *"The integrity of the upright shall guide them: but the perverseness of transgressors shall destroy them... The righteousness of the perfect shall*

direct his way: but the wicked shall fall by his own wickedness. The righteousness of the upright shall deliver them: but transgressors shall be taken in their own naughtiness... As righteousness tendeth to life: so he that pursueth evil pursueth it to his own death." Proverbs 11:3,5,6,19.

"For the wages of sin is death; but the gift of God is eternal life through Jesus Christ our Lord." Romans 6:23.

God Is Not In The Business Of Condemnation

Sin, itself, condemns and destroys. In the full presence of God's purity the unrepentant sinner's own conscience would be so crushed by its guilt that the result would be death.

"For God so loved the world, that he gave his only begotten Son, that whosoever believeth in him should not perish, but have everlasting life. For God sent not his Son into the world to condemn the world; but that the world through him might be saved. He that believeth on him is not condemned: but he that believeth not is condemned already, because he hath not believed in the name of the only begotten Son of God. And this is the condemnation, that light is come into the world, and men loved darkness rather than light, because their deeds were evil. For every one that doeth evil hateth the light, neither cometh to the light, lest his deeds should be reproved.But he that doeth truth cometh to the light, that his deeds may be made manifest, that they are wrought in God." John 3:16-21.

"To wit, that God was in Christ, reconciling the world unto himself, not imputing their trespasses unto them; and hath committed unto us the word of reconciliation." 2 Cor. 5:19

"And said to the mountains and rocks, Fall on us, and hide us from the face of him that sitteth on the throne, and from the wrath of the Lamb: For the great day of his wrath is come; and who shall be able to stand?" Rev. 6:16-17

"He hath not dealt with us after our sins; nor rewarded us according to our iniquities." Psalm 103:10

God is therefore a consuming fire to sin because either His love banishes sin from the contrite and repentant soul or the guilt of sin crushes the soul to death when His wonderful, gracious love is fully manifested to the unrepentant sinner.

"For godly sorrow worketh repentance to salvation not to be repented of: but the sorrow of the world worketh death." 2 Cor. 7:10.

And so we see that God's eternal love is all-conquering. We can do nothing against the truth but for the truth. Love never fails. God's infinite love, compassion and goodness, His absolute selflessness evokes either of two responses.

Either the soul repents and accepts God's love and righteousness, which is eternal life; or the soul rejects God's love and righteousness and thereby cuts itself off from God and that produces the second death.

God's Power And Authority Vindicated

God has such infinite and absolute power, life and authority that those who depart from Him destroy themselves. No one else can "destroy" his enemies like that.

This sets God apart from all others. God overcomes evil with good; hatred with love; violence with peace; death with life; force and hurt with kindness and gentleness.

On the cross Jesus took all the hurt, all the abuse, all the cruelty, all the hatred, all the ridicule and scorn. He took all our sin and its crushing guilt. Yet never, in even a single thought, did he retaliate. He loved His tormentors and longed for their salvation. He prayed for their forgiveness. In dying for us He triumphed over Satan! What love! What a God!

Our response to God's love determines our destiny, either for eternal life or eternal death.

"Therefore I will judge you, O house of Israel, every one according to his ways, saith the Lord God. Repent, and turn yourselves from all your transgressions; so iniquity shall not be your ruin. Cast away from you all your transgressions, whereby ye have transgressed; and make you a new heart and a new spirit: for why will ye die, O house of Israel? For I have no pleasure in the death of him that dieth, saith the Lord God: wherefore turn yourselves, and live ye." Ezekiel 18:30-32.

"Who is a God like unto thee, that pardoneth iniquity, and passeth by the transgression of the remnant of his heritage? he retaineth not his anger for ever, because he delighteth in mercy. He will turn again, he will have compassion upon us; he will subdue our iniquities; and thou wilt cast all their sins into the depths of the sea. Thou wilt perform the truth to Jacob, and the mercy to Abraham, which thou hast sworn unto our fathers from the days of old." Micah 7:18-20.

We have already learned that Jesus demonstrated His Heavenly Father's character during His earthly ministry.

"For the law was given by Moses, but grace and truth came by Jesus Christ. No man hath seen God at any time; the only begotten Son, which is in the bosom of the Father, he hath declared him." John 1:17, 18.

"This then is the message which we have heard of him, and declare unto you, that God is light, and in him is no darkness at all." 1 John 1:5.

There is a very interesting account in Luke where the disciples actually urged Christ to destroy a whole village of Samaritans because they refused to show Him any hospitality. The disciples thought they had a precedent from the Old Testament scriptures and they quoted the prophet Elijah as their example.

But Jesus rebuked them and actually told them that the spirit of retaliation, the spirit of hurting and destroying those who oppose you, is Satanic, not Divine. In this account Jesus made it clear that God does not stand towards His enemies as the executioner of the penalty of transgression.

"And it came to pass, when the time was come that he should be received up, he stedfastly set his face to go to Jerusalem, And sent messengers before his face: and they went, and entered into a village of the Samaritans, to make ready for him. And they did not receive him, because his face was as though he would go to Jerusalem. And when his disciples James and John saw this, they said, Lord, wilt thou that we command fire to come down from heaven, and consume them, even as Elias did? But he turned, and rebuked them, and said, Ye know not what manner of spirit ye are of. For the Son of man is not come to destroy men's lives, but to save them. And they went to another village." Luke 9:51-56.

"Ye have heard that it hath been said, Thou shalt love thy neighbour, and hate thine enemy. But I say unto you, Love your enemies, bless them that curse you, do good to them that hate you, and pray for them which despitefully use you, and persecute you; That ye may be the children of your Father which is in heaven: for he maketh his sun to rise on the evil and on the good, and sendeth rain on the just and on the unjust. For if ye love them which love you, what reward have ye? do not even the publicans the same? And if ye salute your brethren only, what do ye more than others? do not even the publicans so? Be ye therefore perfect, even as your Father which is in heaven is perfect." Matthew 5:43-48.

Fifteen

Three Outstanding Examples

God is the Protector. It is His restraining power which holds in check the sin-damaged powers of nature, and thereby prevents mankind from passing fully under the malignity of Satan's government of sin.

Though they don't know or don't care, those who don't believe in God have great reason to be thankful for God's mercy and long-suffering in holding in check the cruel, malignant power of Satan's government of sin and the perverted powers of creation on our planet and its solar environs.

Yes, dear reader, God is infinitely merciful, loving, compassionate! He is not willing that any should perish. Destruction is not the result of any change in Him.

> *"For I am the Lord, I change not; therefore ye sons of Jacob are not consumed." Malachi 3:6.*

> *"It is of the Lord's mercies that we are not consumed, because his compassions fail not." Lamentations 3:22.*

But God is also a God of justice. In mercy He comes near to save and to protect. In justice He leaves the rejectors of His mercy to themselves to reap what they have sown.

> *"For a small moment have I forsaken thee; but with great mercies will I gather thee. In a little wrath I hid my face from thee for a moment; but with everlasting kindness will I have mercy on thee, saith the Lord thy Redeemer." Isaiah 54: 7,8.*

> *"Be not deceived; God is not mocked: for whatsoever a man soweth, that shall he also reap. For he that soweth to his flesh shall of the flesh reap*

corruption; but he that soweth to the Spirit shall of the Spirit reap life everlasting." Galatians 6:7,8

God exercises His justice in the hiding of His face. And remember it is sin that hides God's face from us. Sin separates from God and produces death.

"But your iniquities have separated between you and your God, and your sins have hid his face from you, that he will not hear." Isaiah 59:2

"Then when lust hath conceived, it bringeth forth sin: and sin, when it is finished, bringeth forth death." James 1:15.

When men pass the limits of divine forbearance, that is, when their minds are irreversibly made up that they do not want God, all that God can do is to "hide His face", withdraw His protective restraint and leave the rejectors of His mercy to reap the whirlwinds of destruction from the sown winds of sin. The Spirit of God, persistently resisted, is at last withdrawn from the rejectors of God's mercy and there is left no power to control or to protect from the malignant effects of sin.

"O Lord, the hope of Israel, all that forsake thee shall be ashamed, and they that depart from me shall be written in the earth, because they have forsaken the Lord, the fountain of living waters." Jeremiah 17:13.

We shall now turn our attention to three outstanding examples of the exercise of God's justice or wrath and learn more precious lessons about God's wonderful protection on one hand and the malignant nature of sin on the other hand.

One: The Flood

"And God saw that the wickedness of man was great in the earth, and that every imagination of the thoughts of his heart was only evil continually. And it repented the Lord that he had made man on the earth, and it grieved him at his heart. And the Lord said, I will destroy man whom I have created from the face of the earth; both man, and beast, and the creeping thing, and the fowls of the air; for it repenteth me that I have made them... And, behold, I, even I, do bring a flood of waters upon the earth, to destroy all flesh, wherein is the breath of life, from under heaven; and every thing that is in the earth shall die." Gen. 6:5-7 and 17

The language is typically punitive, it plainly states that God said, "I will destroy...." "I, even I, do bring a flood of waters..."

By now we should fully understand how such language is to be interpreted. The intensity of sin was so great that it was actually approaching the critical point of separation from God. We are sure of this from Genesis 6:3 and Job 22:15-17.

> "And the Lord said, My spirit shall not always strive with man, for that he also is flesh: yet his days shall be an hundred and twenty years." Genesis 6:3.

The Spirit of God would continue His work of striving with the antediluvians for only one hundred and twenty years more, (a relatively short time, considering the life-span of humans before the flood).

> "Hast thou marked the old way which wicked men have trodden? Which were cut down out of time, whose foundation was overflown with a flood: Which said unto God, Depart from us: and what can the Almighty do for them?" Job 22: 15-17.

The antediluvians, in every thought and imagination, told God to leave them alone, to depart from them. And when the minds of men are irreversibly fixed against God and they wish God to depart from them, what can God do? The answer is given in Hosea 4:17.

> "Ephraim is joined to idols: let him alone." Hosea 4:17.

The antediluvians reached that critical point in sin at which mercy gave way to wrath. They suffered the hiding of God's face, that terrible separation from God caused by sin.

There is a passage in Isaiah where the **mechanisms** of wrath and mercy are linked to the Flood of Noah.

> "For a small moment have I forsaken thee; but with great mercies will I gather thee. In a little wrath I hid my face from thee for a moment; but with everlasting kindness will I have mercy on thee, saith the Lord thy Redeemer. For this is as the waters of Noah unto me: for as I have sworn that the waters of Noah should no more go over the earth; so have I sworn that I would not be wroth with thee, nor rebuke thee." Isaiah 54: 7,8,9

We have conclusive evidence here that the Antediluvians reached that critical point in rebellion against God when sin separated them irreversibly from God (Isaiah 59:2) but is expressed as: God hiding His face from them, when He forsook them, when He withdrew His Spirit, and when He departed because He was asked to leave. And, as usual, the Bible describes God as doing what He did not prevent.

In order to understand how the Flood happened after God withdrew, we must learn about the special geophysical conditions which existed before the Flood.

On the first day of creation-week the earth was submerged in a vast quantity of water.

> "In the beginning God created the heaven and the earth. And the earth was without form, and void; and darkness was upon the face of the deep. And the Spirit of God moved upon the face of the waters." Genesis 1:1,2

On the second day God divided the vast quantity of water into two separate masses: water on the earth and water above the sky or firmament.

> "And God said, Let there be a firmament in the midst of the waters, and let it divide the waters from the waters. And God made the firmament, and divided the waters which were under the firmament from the waters which were above the firmament: and it was so." Genesis 1:6,7.

On the fourth day God made two great lights, the Sun and the Moon.

> "And God made two great lights; the greater light to rule the day, and the lesser light to rule the night: he made the stars also." Genesis 1:16.

The language here in Genesis 1:16 suggests that the Moon, when it was created, was a self-luminous body—a great light, not a mere reflector. This is confirmed by Isaiah who informs us that when all things shall be restored, the Moon will be as bright as our present Sun and the restored Sun will be seven times brighter.

> "Moreover, the light of the moon shall be as the light of the sun, and the light of the sun shall be sevenfold, as the light of seven days, in the day that the Lord bindeth up the breach of his people, and healeth the stroke of their wound." Isaiah 30:26.

The combined heat of the Sun and Moon supplied more than enough energy to keep the vast quantity of water above the firmament in the vapour state. This vast quantity of water vapour completely surrounded our planet and allowed a mild, beautiful, "air-conditioned" climate all over the earth. They were no frigid north and south poles and no torrid equatorial regions. The temperature was the same all over. The earth's surface was a paradise of beautiful vegetation and the climate was ideal.

In Job 38, God mentioned this cloud or swaddling band of water vapour, that surrounded our planet as a protective garment.

"When I made the cloud the garment thereof, and thick darkness a swaddlingband for it." Job 38:9.

God's infinite power, infinite wisdom and infinite love in His Son through His Spirit maintained that ingenious masterpiece of created geophysical technology in perfect working order.

The antediluvians were blessed with paradise conditions, they were strong, healthy and long-lived, but they rejected God's government of righteousness and as a result wickedness reached unimaginable and unprecedented proportions.

Rain did not fall in the antediluvian world, in fact that was a world so vastly different to our present world that it stretches the mind to grasp it.

All the water on the surface of the planet was in one place and all the dry land mass was in one body—a geographical topography unknown to our present system. During the night as the temperature cooled off, enough condensation occurred to allow a mist or dew to moisten the whole face of the ground. There were no storms, no extremes of climate, no weather disturbances as now exist in our present world. Furthermore, the massive water vapor mantle prevented any beams of sunlight from entering directly into the atmosphere, screening all radiant energy or rays which would have been dangerous to creatures on earth. Man and animals ate fruits and herbs as stated in Genesis 1:29, indeed everything was conducive to health, vigour and longevity.

The warning given by Noah was ridiculed and rejected. Yet for 120 years God's spirit pleaded with the antediluvians.

Because God foreknew the consequences of sin's irreversible separation, He advised Noah to build an ark, and all who had faith enough to go into that ark would have been saved from the flood.

When Noah and his family were safe in the ark, the angel of God closed the door and for seven days **no change appeared: the antediluvians did not realize that probation was closed, that God had withdrawn and that the Sun and Moon were undergoing drastic changes.** Then 7 days after Noah entered the ark, *"all the springs of the great deep burst forth and the floodgates of the heavens were opened. And rain fell on the earth forty days and forty nights."* Genesis 7:11, 12 (NIV). Yes, the vast quantity of water above the firmament came down; the Sun had been reduced to its present state, the Moon had gone out. The controlling protective, sustaining power over the elements was no longer present and one great upheaval occurred. **It was the day of judgment for that corrupt civilization. They understood too late that the wages of sin is death. They did not want God and He departed from them.** The Apostle Peter refers to the great change that took place, in 2 Peter 3:3-7.

> *"Knowing this first, that there shall come in the last days scoffers, walking after their own lusts, And saying, Where is the promise of his coming? for since the fathers fell asleep, all things continue as they were from the beginning of the creation. For this they willingly are ignorant of, that by the word of God the heavens were of old, and the earth standing out of the water and in the water: Whereby the world that then was, being overflowed with water, perished: But the heavens and the earth, which are now, by the same word are kept in store, reserved unto fire against the day of judgment and perdition of ungodly men." 2 Peter 3:3-7.*

After the flood the world was so different, so inferior to what it was before! The burial of the immense forests gave rise to the formation of coal and oil, volcanoes and earthquakes. **Thus the next time God withdraws there will be fiery destruction.** 2 Peter 3:7.

The Sun, Moon, the entire Solar System and even beyond were profoundly affected by the terrible separation from God, which caused the Flood of Noah's day. Astronomical pictures of the moon and planets of the present Solar System show chaotic surfaces with volcanic activity and fierce wind storms, in other words, the forces of nature on the planets are as disordered as they are here on earth. We know that God made a perfect creation in the beginning so wherever we see disorder we know it is the result of the sin problem on earth.

There can never again be a global flood as in Noah's day because the vast quantity of water vapour, which was above the firmament, came down at the Flood. Direct beams of light have since then been entering our atmosphere and whenever such direct beams pass through an area of cloudiness there is refraction of the light producing the spectrum of colours found in white light. This is called the *rainbow*. Whenever we see it we should remember the changes in geography which occurred at the Flood.

> *"And I will establish my covenant with you; neither shall all flesh be cut off any more by the waters of a flood; neither shall there any more be a flood to destroy the earth... And it shall come to pass, when I bring a cloud over the earth, that the bow shall be seen in the cloud: And I will*

remember my covenant, which is between me and you and every living creature of all flesh; and the waters shall no more become a flood to destroy all flesh." Genesis 9: 11, 14, 15

Two: Sodom And Gomorrah (Genesis Chapters 18 and 19)

Sodom and Gomorrah were two of five cities in the plentifully watered and very fertile plain of the River Jordan. We are first introduced to these cities in Genesis 13 when Lot and Abram parted ways and Lot chose to live in the plain of Jordan.

"And Abram said unto Lot, Let there be no strife, I pray thee, between me and thee, and between my herdmen and thy herdmen; for we be brethren. Is not the whole land before thee? separate thyself, I pray thee, from me: if thou wilt take the left hand, then I will go to the right; or if thou depart to the right hand, then I will go to the left. And Lot lifted up his eyes, and beheld all the plain of Jordan, that it was well watered every where, before the Lord destroyed Sodom and Gomorrah, even as the garden of the Lord, like the land of Egypt, as thou comest unto Zoar. Then Lot chose him all the plain of Jordan; and Lot journeyed east: and they separated themselves the one from the other. Abram dwelled in the land of Canaan, and Lot dwelled in the cities of the plain, and pitched his tent toward Sodom." Genesis 13:8-12.

Right away we are told about the character of the inhabitants of Sodom.

"But the men of Sodom were wicked and sinners before the Lord exceedingly." Gen. 13:13.

The five cities of the plain are mentioned in Genesis 14 when they were collectively under a military attack by four kings led by the king of Elam. The battle took place in the very fertile plain of Jordan in an area called the Vale of Siddim (which is now the salt sea).

"And it came to pass in the days of Amraphel king of Shinar, Arioch king of Ellasar, Chedorlaomer king of Elam, and Tidal king of nations; That these made war with Bera king of Sodom, and with Birsha king of Gomorrah, Shinab king of Admah, and Shemeber king of Zeboiim, and the king of Bela, which is Zoar. All these were joined together in the vale of Siddim, which is the salt sea." Genesis 14:1-3.

Some very important information is given in verse 10.

"And the vale of Siddim was full of slimepits; and the kings of Sodom and Gomorrah fled, and fell there; and they that remained fled to the mountain." Genesis 14:10.

The vale of Siddim, the beautiful fertile valley surrounding the cities of the plain, **was full of slime pits.** The slime pits oozed out asphalt from beneath the earth's surface. Obviously this was an area where immense amounts of trees had been buried during the Flood resulting in the formation of petroleum products.

The cities of the plain were sitting, as it were, on a natural "time-bomb" and they neither knew nor cared.

God's protection, God's blessings, God's mercy sustained the cities of the plain maintaining life and fertility. But their probation was fast closing.

In Genesis 18, Abraham was visited by three Heavenly Beings. One was the Son of God! Abraham addressed Him as LORD meaning Jehovah.

The LORD announced to Abraham and Sarah that the son of promise would be born a year later and then He announced the fact that probation for the cities of the plain was rapidly closing. The LORD revealed to Abraham that Divine Judgement would be pronounced and executed upon Sodom and Gomorrah and their neighbouring cities.

The actual description of the execution of Divine Judgement is written down in Genesis 19: 23-29.

"The sun was risen upon the earth when Lot entered into Zoar. Then the Lord rained upon Sodom and upon Gomorrah brimstone and fire from the Lord out of heaven; And he overthrew those cities, and all the plain, and all the inhabitants of the cities, and that which grew upon the ground. But his wife looked back from behind him, and she became a pillar of salt. And Abraham gat up early in the morning to the place where he stood before the Lord: And he looked toward Sodom and Gomorrah, and toward all the land of the plain, and beheld, and, lo, the smoke of the country went up as the smoke of a furnace. And it came to pass, when God destroyed the cities of the plain, that God remembered Abraham, and sent Lot out of the midst of the overthrow, when he overthrew the cities in the which Lot dwelt." Gen. 19:23-29.

Again the language is clear: it says that the LORD rained upon Sodom and Gomorrah brimstone and fire from the LORD out of heaven. He destroyed, He overthrew those cities!

Does scripture give us the correct interpretation of such language in terms of the mechanism by which those cities were destroyed?

Yes!

Our first evidence comes from Deuteronomy chapter 29 where Moses reminded the Israelites of God's covenant with them, the blessings of obedience and the curses of disobedience which are listed in Chapter 28.

He particularly mentioned in Deut 29:18,19 the sins of idolatry, false worship and boastful defiance.

Moses then clearly outlined the punishments which would befall the people and their land in Deuteronomy 29: 20-29. Let us consider verse 23.

> *"And that the whole land thereof is brimstone, and salt, and burning, that it is not sown, nor beareth, nor any grass groweth therein, like the overthrow of Sodom, and Gomorrah, Admah, and Zeboim, which the Lord overthrew in his anger, and in his wrath:" Deut. 29:23.*

Here Moses clearly stated that God would do to them like He did to Sodom and Gomorrah, Admah and Zeboim. He would overthrow the land with fire and brimstone and salt. This would be the result of God's anger kindled against the land.

> *"And the anger of the Lord was kindled against this land, to bring upon it all the curses that are written in this book:" Deut. 29:27.*

But over in Deuteronomy 31: 16-18 God explained the mechanism of wrath.

> *"And the Lord said unto Moses, Behold, thou shalt sleep with thy fathers; and this people will rise up, and go a whoring after the gods of the strangers of the land, whither they go to be among them, and will forsake me, and break my covenant which I have made with them. Then my anger shall be kindled against them in that day, and I will forsake them, and I will hide my face from them, and they shall be devoured, and many evils and troubles shall befall them; so that they will say in that day, Are not these evils come upon us, because our God is not among us? And I will surely hide my face in that day for all the evils which they shall have wrought, in that they are turned unto other gods." Deut. 31:16-18.*

Therefore the overthrow of the land with fire and brimstone and salt would be the result of God forsaking them and hiding His face from them.

Obviously then the sins of the cities of the plain reached that point where the inhabitants passed the limits of divine forbearance, their minds were irreversibly fixed against God. They did not want God and God withdrew from them. They did not realize that God's Spirit through His angels was holding in check the sin-perverted forces of nature around them. When God let go there was nothing to prevent the fiery explosion which destroyed them.

This is further confirmed in Amos 4:9-11, where God rehearsed some of the curses with which Israel was smitten. He told them:

> "I have overthrown some of you, as God overthrew Sodom and Gomorrah, and ye were as a firebrand plucked out of the burning: yet have ye not returned unto me, saith the Lord." Amos 4:11.

It is clear then that the mechanism of Sodom's overthrow was the same mechanism stated in Deuteronomy 31:16-18. Our third confirmatory evidence is written down in Hosea 11:7,8.

> "And my people are bent to backsliding from me: though they called them to the most High, none at all would exalt him. How shall I give thee up, Ephraim? how shall I deliver thee, Israel? how shall I make thee as Admah? how shall I set thee as Zeboim? mine heart is turned within me, my repentings are kindled together." Hosea 11:7,8.

God asked Ephraim and Israel: "How shall I give thee up? "How shall I deliver thee?" And in giving Israel up He would be making her as Admah and Zeboim, the cities of the plain. Therefore the cities of the plain were "given up" or "delivered up". And they were **delivered to trouble and commotion**.

> "Wherefore the wrath of the Lord was upon Judah and Jerusalem, and he hath delivered them to trouble, to astonishment, and to hissing, as ye see with your eyes. For, lo, our fathers have fallen by the sword, and our sons and our daughters and our wives are in captivity for this." 2 Chron. 29: 8,9.

In Romans 1, Paul explains that God's wrath is exercised when He gives up those who reject His mercy. (See Romans 1:18, 24, 26, 28, see Chapter 7). Sodom and Gomorrah and the cities of the plain were **given up** by God. He **hid His face** from them. He **forsook them**. He **withdrew His protection** and they were consumed by a fiery explosion.

One last point must be clarified.

The fire with brimstone is described as falling from God out of heaven. We met a similar term in Job 1:16 when it is said that "the fire of God is fallen from heaven...." But such fire resulted when God handed over Job's possessions to Satan, Job 1:12. In other words the "fire of God fallen from heaven" is caused by sin's separation from God.

Three: The Destruction Of Jerusalem In A.D 70

In the parable of the Wedding Garment in Matthew 22:1-14, Jesus described the fate of Jerusalem in verse 7.

> *"But when the king heard thereof, he was wroth: and he sent forth his armies, and destroyed those murderers, and burned up their city."* Matt. 22:7.

Notice the language. God (the king) was wroth and He (God) sent forth His armies, and He (God) destroyed those murderers and (He) burned up their city. God is described as the One who **directly** and **personally** performed the destruction of the people and the burning of the city.

But by now we have mastered the principles of interpretation. We know that such language must be correctly understood not according to the apparent meaning of the language but according to the deeper principles of allowing the Bible to explain itself and therefore to explain the mechanism by which the destruction occurred.

In Luke 21:20-24 Jesus predicted the destruction of Jerusalem. Listen to what He said in verses 22, 23.

> *"For these be the days of vengeance, that all things which are written may be fulfilled. But woe unto them that are with child, and to them that give suck, in those days! for there shall be great distress in the land, and wrath upon this people."* Luke 21:22, 23.

Two points of special significance are in these verses.

First is His statement that the time of Jerusalem's destruction would be *"the days of vengeance, that all things which are written be fulfilled."* (verse 22). Where was Jerusalem's destruction written down long before the Messiah's birth? It was written down in Deuteronomy, Chapter 28, the chapter of the blessings and the curses, verses 49-57.

The second point is His statement in verse 23 that *wrath would be upon the people.* In other words Jerusalem, in its destruction in A.D 70, suffered the vengeance of God, the wrath of God.

All we need to do now is to carefully examine the scriptures to find out the precise mechanism by which the "vengeance" and "wrath" of God caused the destruction. Incontrovertible evidence is found in Matthew 23:37, 38.

> *"O Jerusalem, Jerusalem, thou that killest the prophets, and stonest them which are sent unto thee, how often would I have gathered thy children together, even as a hen gathereth her chickens under her*

wings, and ye would not! Behold, your house is left unto you desolate."
Matthew 23:37, 38.

In these verses Jesus explained that He longed to save and protect Jerusalem, to keep her children under the protective wings of His mercy and grace, but the Jewish Nation rejected all His mercy, all His love, all of His saving grace.

And Jesus told them that their house would be left unto them desolate. This means He would have to **give them up**, **withdraw** His protection and blessing and **leave them** to reap the consequences of centuries of repeated apostasy.

When, at the crucifixion of Christ the Jews shouted out "Away with this man and release unto us Barabbas:"

> *"And they cried out all at once, saying, Away with this man, and release unto us Barabbas:" Luke 23:18,*

When they cried out, *"Away with him, away with him … we have no king but Caesar,"* (John 19:15), they closed their National probation, and sealed their fate by completely rejecting the only One who could bless, save and protect them from evil.

In A.D 70 Jerusalem suffered that terrible separation from God's protective mercy; she was **given up**. God handed her over to the kings of her choice—Caesar the Roman king who was under the control of Satan the king of evil.

Jerusalem suffered the retributive vengeance, the awful justice, the terrible wrath of God. And what was the mechanism? It was consistently the same as in every other case. God exercised His wrath by **withdrawing** His blessings and His protection and by **handing** Jerusalem over, **giving her up** to reap the **whirlwind** from the **wind** she had been sowing for centuries!

But this was exactly what God had told Moses in Deuteronomy 31:16-18.

All the evils, **every single one of them** would befall the Israelites because they rejected God and He left them to the consequences of their choice. Here is Deuteronomy 31:16-18 as translated in the Today's English Version of the Bible.

> *"The Lord said to Moses, 'You will soon die, and after your death the people will become unfaithful to me and break the covenant that I made with them. They will abandon me and worship the pagan gods of the land they are about to enter. When that happens, I will become angry with them; I will abandon them, and they will be destroyed. Many terrible*

disasters will come upon them, and then they will realize that these things are happening to them because I, their God, am no longer with them. And I will refuse to help them then, because they have done evil and worshiped other gods." Deut 31:16-18 (TEV).

In 586 B.C Jerusalem had also suffered "punishment" for her sins. Nebuchadnezzar king of Babylon invaded and destroyed the city and the Jews started their 70-year Babylonian captivity. Jeremiah's description is recorded in Jeremiah 25:9-11.

"Behold, I will send and take all the families of the north, saith the Lord, and Nebuchadnezzar the king of Babylon, my servant, and will bring them against this land, and against the inhabitants thereof, and against all these nations round about, and will utterly destroy them, and make them an astonishment, and an hissing, and perpetual desolations. Moreover, I will take from them the voice of mirth, and the voice of gladness, the voice of the bridegroom, and the voice of the bride, the sound of the millstones, and the light of the candle. And this whole land shall be a desolation, and an astonishment; and these nations shall serve the king of Babylon seventy years." Jer. 25:9-11.

Notice the language. God said:

"I will … bring Nebuchadnezzar against the inhabitants … and I will utterly destroy."

In Ezra 5:12 the same event is described and Ezra explained that God exercised His wrath by giving up Jerusalem and the Jews into the hand of Nebuchadnezzar who destroyed the city and took the people captive.

"But after that our fathers had provoked the God of heaven unto wrath, he gave them into the hand of Nebuchadnezzar the king of Babylon, the Chaldean, who destroyed this house, and carried the people away into Babylon." Ezra 5:12.

In each case of punishment God had exercised His wrath by **withdrawing** His protection and **giving them** up to their enemies. In fact they destroyed themselves by forsaking the Lord.

"Israel, you brought this on yourself! You deserted me, the Lord your God, while I was leading you along the way. What do you think you will gain by going to Egypt to drink water from the Nile? What do you think you will gain by going to Assyria to drink water from the Euphrates? Your own

evil will punish you, and your turning from me will condemn you. You will learn how bitter and wrong it is to abandon me, the Lord your God, and no longer to remain loyal to me. I, the Sovereign Lord Almighty, have spoken." Jer. 2:17-19 (TEV).

The prophet Hosea also expressed the fact that all Israel's punishments were caused by separation from God through persistence in sin.

"O Israel, return unto the Lord thy God; for thou hast fallen by thine iniquity." Hosea 14:1.

"O Israel, thou hast destroyed thyself; but in me is thine help." Hosea 13:9

"Woe unto them! for they have fled from me: destruction unto them! because they have transgressed against me: though I have redeemed them, yet they have spoken lies against me." Hosea 7:13.

"Ye have plowed wickedness, ye have reaped iniquity; ye have eaten the fruit of lies: because thou didst trust in thy way, in the multitude of thy mighty men. Therefore shall a tumult arise among thy people, and all thy fortresses shall be spoiled, as Shalman spoiled Betharbel in the day of battle: the mother was dashed in pieces upon her children. So shall Bethel do unto you because of your great wickedness: in a morning shall the king of Israel utterly be cut off." Hosea 10:13-15.

God had always been willing and eager to heal their backsliding. His love is unconditional. His heart yearned for their salvation.

"When Israel was a child, then I loved him, and called my son out of Egypt... I drew them with cords of a man, with bands of love: and I was to them as they that take off the yoke on their jaws, and I laid meat unto them." Hosea 11:1,4

"O Israel, return unto the Lord thy God; for thou hast fallen by thine iniquity... I will heal their backsliding, I will love them freely: for mine anger is turned away from him." Hosea 14:1,4

When Jerusalem rejected her Messiah, she filled up her cup of iniquity and cut herself off from God. In A.D 70 God **gave her up**, He exercised His wrath in the same unchanging consistency as always, He **withdrew** His blessings and His protective mercy and left her to reap the destruction and calamities which were the inevitable consequences of her separation from Him.

Sixteen

Answers To Objections

Any belief or doctrine which is popular and which by a long tradition has become entrenched in the minds of the masses of people, is difficult for the human mind to let go, even when shown to be error.

The blackening of God's character by Satan started in Heaven and therefore a false picture of the character of our Heavenly Father is the oldest of all errors.

Moreover, Satan mounts an "all out" attack whenever the light on God's true character starts to penetrate the darkness. We should not be surprised at this. Satan's success in his work of deceiving souls depends on his painting a false picture of our Heavenly Father.

At the first Advent of Christ the Jewish people had a terribly wrong concept of God. Their misinterpretation of their scriptures had led them to believe that God was a stern Judge, an exacting tyrant who loved His friends but hated His enemies. They pictured God as One who delighted in the destruction of His enemies.

As a result of this wrong concept, this false image of God, their religious motivation was one of fear. And so they worked very hard to earn His favour and to appease His wrath. They multiplied their own rules in order to ensure that the law of God was kept while all the time they were so afraid of God that their souls became empty of love. They became so selfish in motive, that theirs became a religion of rigid legal orthodoxy devoid of any saving virtue.

The picture of God's character which Jesus gave was so different from their tradition they refused to believe that He was the Son of God.

"And the light shineth in darkness; and the darkness comprehended it not... He was in the world, and the world was made by him, and the world knew him not. He came unto his own, and his own received him not... For the law was given by Moses, but grace and truth came by Jesus Christ. No man hath seen God at any time; the only begotten Son, which is in the bosom of the Father, he hath declared him." John 1:5, 10, 11, 17, 18.

They were looking for a Messiah who would use violent force to overthrow the Romans and put the Jewish Nation in the top spot of world glory. But Jesus disappointed their worldly hopes. Instead He revealed God to be a God of mercy who rejoices over one soul who is saved. He explained to them that what God desired most was their love and trust which would enable them to receive genuine righteousness as a gift and therefore experience victory over sin.

Jesus swept away their meaningless legalistic traditions and showed them that only love could fulfill God's law.

The Jews so hated the true revelation of God's character which Jesus gave that they called Him a deceiver (Matthew 27:63), and Beelzebub (Matthew 12:24). They persecuted Him and ultimately crucified Him!

Whenever and wherever the true light of God's character starts to shine, Satan moves religious people to rise up in fear, unbelief and hatred against the truth.

The Jewish Nation was the true church in Jesus' day and oh how terribly they hated and rejected Him who was the Truth, while claiming that they were defending religious orthodoxy.

"Ye are of your father the devil, and the lusts of your father ye will do. He was a murderer from the beginning, and abode not in the truth, because there is no truth in him. When he speaketh a lie, he speaketh of his own: for he is a liar, and the father of it. And because I tell you the truth, ye believe me not." John 8:44, 45.

There is nothing that Satan fears so much as the revelation of the true light of God's character because such light exposes the worthlessness and malignant nature of his government of sin in contrast to God's wonderfully benign character of love, righteousness and truth. And remember perfect love dispels all fear.

"There is no fear in love; perfect love drives out all fear. So then, love has not been made perfect in anyone who is afraid, because fear has to do with punishment." 1 John 4: 18, (TEV).

Those who oppose the true light on the character of God raise a number of charges or objections which we shall now consider.

1 It is being charged that this new doctrine teaches that God is so loving He will not punish the impenitent sinner.

Nothing could be further from the truth. Any honest reader of this book will see that such an objection is baseless.

In fact this **true** message of the character of God teaches that the impenitent will most definitely be punished and will suffer the ultimate wages of sin, which is the second death. What this message teaches is the **true mechanism** by which the punishment or destruction occurs.

God is not arbitrary, He is absolute in all His ways. Those who reject His **mercy** will most definitely suffer His **wrath.**

This message explains the true meaning of wrath and the mechanism by which it operates.

God has given to His intelligent creatures genuine freedom.

If they choose God's government they receive eternal life in Christ.

If they reject God's government they cut themselves off from the only Source of life. Ultimately Satan, his demons and all impenitent humans will suffer destruction by fire and end up in the second death. But such a fate will be the inevitable result of separation from God by sin.

In almost every area of religious belief there are those who go to extremes and therefore end up in error. Anyone who teaches that the impenitent will not be ultimately destroyed is not a believer in the true message of the character of God.

2 The Bible says that God destroys, that He has destroyed sinners in the past and will destroy them, finally, in the end. Therefore why do you say that God does not destroy?

The reader is referred back to Chapters 7 and 12). Bible language in reference to God must be correctly understood.

For example true Christianity does not teach that God hardens the hearts of men and makes them impenitent. On the contrary, true Christianity teaches that God does not harden men's hearts, He does **not** make people impenitent. In fact it is God's goodness which leads to repentance (Romans 2:4)

So the question could be asked, "Why do Christians teach that God does not harden men's hearts when the Bible clearly states that He hardened

Pharaoh's heart and hardened the hearts of Israel's enemies and sends strong delusion to make people believe a lie?" The reason is that true Christianity interprets these statements correctly to mean that God's Spirit, persistently resisted, ultimately leaves the soul encased in its own hardness and deceived by the lies and falsehoods it has chosen.

Similarly, as has been explained in earlier chapters, the statement "God destroys" means **that He leaves the rejectors of His mercy to reap the destruction which sin causes by separating sinners from His protection.**

3   The Bible says there is one lawgiver who is able to save and to destroy (James 4:12). What do you say to that?

What a wonderful text in James 4:12. The reader is referred back to chapter 14. God's ability to destroy is not arbitrary, it is absolute; therefore those who surrender to His redemptive work in Jesus Christ are saved whereas those who reject the free gift of salvation separate themselves from the Source of Life and God will eventually give them up to reap the ultimate consequences of sin. Only He can destroy in this way.

4   Careful study proves that God withdraws and leaves the rejectors of His mercy to reap destruction, but that is only one method by which God destroys, surely in other cases He personally and directly kills His opponents.

This objection is interesting in more ways than one.

First of all, before the light on God's character came, **every single statement** about "God destroying" was understood to mean a direct and personal act of God to kill the sinner. Then came the light on God's character and the mechanism of destruction became clear.

In Bible exegesis (interpretative analysis) the correct method is to find the underlying **principles** and use those principles to interpret any **statement**. Statements do not change principles, rather principles **must interpret statements**.

Where is the evidence that God has other methods of destroying? What is meant by a method of destroying anyway?

God withdraws His protection because the sinner has irreversibly rejected His mercy and the separation from God leaves the sinner exposed to any calamity which the unrestrained forces of evil might produce. The calamity is called the method of destruction but the underlying mechanism is always God's withdrawal from the sinner i.e. sin's separation of the sinner from God.

Every time there is an explanation in the Bible for a "God destroys" statement, it is the mechanism of withdrawal that produces calamity. Obviously the correct exegesis is that God's withdrawal is the consistent underlying mechanism because God is changeless (see Chapter 12). Those who argue otherwise must bear the burden of proof which proof they cannot supply. All they do is to quote a statement of destruction by God and argue that it is a direct act. It is like reading statements of fire burning forever and ever. Once the underlying principle is found we should know how to interpret such statements. Yet some people will want to say that some of such statements may literally mean eternal fire.

The point is they have rejected the underlying principle of correct interpretation. Opponents of the message usually spend considerable time searching the Old Testament for examples of destruction by God. When an explanation is given for one they search for another and so on and on.

We should remember that in every doctrine there are some perplexing statements but we should make our decision on the **weight** of evidence.

The Bible makes it clear that **all** the evils which befell His ancient people had the same mechanism. They forsook Him, and He withdrew from them and gave them up to reap the consequences of their choice. Read it again in Deut. 31:16-18.

Consider, for example, the judgement or punishment which God pronounced upon king David after his double transgression of adultery and murder. It is written down in 2 Samuel 12:10-12.

> *"Now therefore the sword shall never depart from thine house; because thou hast despised me, and hast taken the wife of Uriah the Hittite to be thy wife. Thus saith the Lord, Behold, I will raise up evil against thee out of thine own house, and I will take thy wives before thine eyes, and give them unto thy neighbour, and he shall lie with thy wives in the sight of this sun. For thou didst it secretly: but I will do this thing before all Israel, and before the sun." 2 Samuel 12:10-12*

Notice the language again. God said:

> *"I will raise up evil against thee ...."*

> *"I will take thy wives... and give them to thy neighbour."*

Does God take men's wives and give them to others? How does God raise up evil? What does the language mean?

It means that God would, in a measure, withdraw His protective restraint and allow David to reap the evil consequences of his terrible sin.

In Chapter 12 we proved the important principle that:

> **Whenever any text of scripture describes God as causing, doing, or sending evil or calamity, it *must be interpreted* to mean that God allows or permits the evil by withdrawing his protection and restraint.**

5 Some opponents charge that this character of God message is a species of pantheism.

Pantheism is a false doctrine which teaches that God is merely an essence pervading and indwelling every thing animate or inanimate. In contrast, true Christianity teaches that God is a Personal Being whose existence is above and beyond the creation. He sustains His creation by His Spirit.

When God withdraws His sustaining, protective grace from any part of creation, that part must collapse to destruction because the creation cannot sustain itself.

The character of God message proves that pantheism is wrong and safeguards the believer against pantheism.

To say that the **mechanism of withdrawal** is pantheistic is a desperate attempt to discredit God's truth. Does God teach pantheism?

NO!

And God told the Israelites that all the evils which would befall them would be caused by His **withdrawal** from them. (Deut. 31:16-18).

6 The doctrine that God is harmless makes Him look weak.

This charge is founded upon ignorance. Far from making God look weak, this message shows that God is infinite in power.

So absolutely, infinitely powerful is our God that those who depart from Him write themselves off. Only He can destroy without force because He alone is the Source of life. Those who reject Him cut themselves off from life.

7 This character of God message makes people believe that God and Satan are in partnership.

When God withdraws His restraint from the forces of evil, Satan is as helpless as anyone else to stop calamity. In the very end, when He withdraws from Satan, he (Satan) will be burned into non-existence. So to say that this message puts God and Satan in partnership is a ridiculous falsehood.

God invites us all to reason logically and truthfully. Those who trust, surrender and obey will live, those who rebel will be given up to the sword of destruction.

> *"Come now, and let us reason together, saith the Lord: though your sins be as scarlet, they shall be as white as snow; though they be red like crimson, they shall be as wool. If ye be willing and obedient, ye shall eat the good of the land: But if ye refuse and rebel, ye shall be devoured with the sword: for the mouth of the Lord hath spoken it." Isaiah 1:18, 19, 20.*

> *"O Lord, the hope of Israel, all that forsake thee shall be ashamed, and they that depart from me shall be written in the earth, because they have forsaken the Lord, the fountain of living waters." Jeremiah 17:13.*

8 God gave Samson the strength to destroy the Philistines. And Elijah slew the prophets of Baal in the name of God. Therefore God kills.

In chapter 11 of this book it was shown that Israel in her gradual and progressive departure from God's ways chose to have her own civil punishments, her own military system and eventually her own monarchial system. Israel chose the way of the "sword." God simply gave the best instructions within the context of Israel's chosen methods of operating. Israel's methods of operating were not God's methods and did not reflect His character. To prove this, remember that Samuel anointed Israel's first king in THE NAME OF THE LORD but God had already indicated that their having kings was not His will for them. Yet when they were fixed in their choice of a king, He directed Samuel to anoint king Saul in the NAME OF THE LORD.

They did all their operations in the name of the Lord and in the strength of the Lord, not because the particular operation was God's way but because God worked along with them in their chosen methods, giving them the best counsel and success in their wrong choices, while all the time seeking to bring them back to His perfect ways and will! It was His willingness to still work along with them, notwithstanding their wrong ways of doing things, that reflected His character of patience, mercy and love.

Moreover, Ahab and Jezebel had led Israel into apostasy and Baal worship. The true prophets of God were persecuted and many people were enlisted to be prophets of Baal. It was as a direct result of departure from God that destruction befell the prophets of Baal by the method of execution. Destruction befell Jezebel and Ahab in warfare. All these evils, every one, came upon them by the mechanism written down in Deut. 31:16-18.

9 Jesus was the One who fully revealed the character of God yet it was Jesus who said in Matthew 10:28, *"And fear not them which kill the body, but are not able to kill the soul: but rather fear him which is able to destroy both soul and body in hell."* Here Jesus plainly taught that God will kill soul and body in hell.

The words of Jesus like God's words in the Bible must be interpreted by the same rules of interpretation by which all scriptures are interpreted.

If we are saying that these words of Jesus need no interpretation we will run into trouble with the parable of Luke 16:19-31, where His words state that Lazarus was taken to heaven when he died and the rich man went to hell after death.

They are those who use this parable to support the teaching of immediate rewards at death and the natural immortality of the soul. But this parable has to be correctly interpreted.

In the Lord's prayer in Matthew 6:13 Jesus asked His Father not to lead us into temptation.

Does God tempt people? What is meant by "leading us not into temptation?" Is God the Source of temptation? Obviously all scripture, including statements of God or Jesus, must be correctly interpreted by absolute principles of interpretation.

Also in John 11:26, Jesus told the Jews "whosoever liveth and believeth in Me shall never die." Again, this statement must be correctly understood!

The key point is that Jesus **demonstrated** in His life and, supremely, in His death, the character of God and the mechanism of wrath. He was separated from His Father by our sins and died our second death for us. This means that the second death is caused by the ultimate separation from God by sin. God will "destroy" soul and body in the end by **withdrawing** His life-sustaining grace from those who do not want Him and they will be killed by that terrible and terminal separation from God by sin.

10 Since God made natural powers and laws like the power of gravity, if a person jumps off a high building or is thrown from a great height and is killed, the Lord has done it because the Lord made the power of gravity. Since God made the universe with all its laws, He is responsible for and is the cause of the results of breaking natural law. So the cigarette smoker who gets lung cancer believes that the lung cancer is caused by God!

In making the universe God, of necessity, had to make powers and systems (called natural laws) for the perfect well-being of His creatures.

The power of gravity is absolutely essential for life and order on our planet. If there were no law of gravity everything on earth would float away into outer space. If the law of gravity were not constant in quantity and direction we could go to sleep on our beds at night and wake up stuck on to our roofs next morning!

God is a God of order, precision and precise mathematical exactness. God's absolute, eternal moral law, which is a transcript of His nature and character, must guide His intelligent creatures in their use of the natural powers of creation.

Power without righteousness (law) is destructive.

Wisdom or Righteousness without power is useless.

The righteous and wise use of power is life maintaining.

God has made us all free moral agents. You can use the natural powers of your muscles to help an old lady carry her load or you can use these same powers to hit and injure her.

When you use your natural muscular powers to hurt her it would be manifestly absurd to say that God has hurt her. He has not.

The perversion or transgression of law causes hurt and death.

The correct use of all law, moral and natural, is life maintaining. The violation of any law produces disastrous results. It is not the righteous law but its violation, which produces destructive results. God never uses His power unrighteously. When men transgress moral or natural law it is the transgression which produces the pain and suffering and death; not God, not God's laws. Transgression of law is not law, it is sin.

Furthermore, this charge is as sinister as it is absurd because it is really blaming God for sin and all of its consequences and this is precisely the charge which Satan laid against God in the beginning.

Notice too that when God approached Adam and Eve immediately after the Fall (Genesis 3) each of them had an excuse.

When God asked Adam if he had eaten of the forbidden tree he blamed Eve and he blamed God since God had given him Eve. He told God, "The woman whom **thou gavest to be with me**, she gave me of the tree, and I did eat." Genesis 3:12.

Using God's wonderfully created natural gifts and laws to blame God for the results of transgression is an error as old as the earth and must be exposed not only as absurd but as echoing Satan's unreasonable and illogical charges against our loving and gracious Creator.

As we learned earlier, Adam's one act of disobedience sold out our planet with its created powers and systems of nature to Satan's government of sin. Sin perverted these powers by separating them from God's perfect righteousness. God, by His mercy through the Holy Spirit and His angels, is holding in check the perverted powers of nature. The ongoing separation of these powers from God's mercy by sin will produce increasingly frequent and severe natural calamities and disaster. In the end-time Satan will say that God is causing these calamities because people are neglecting Sunday worship when in fact these calamities will be the inevitable results of transgressing the Ten Commandments.

It has already been clearly shown by the study of Job that evil, sickness, suffering, calamities and death are the results of the work of Satan and sin when God's protective hedge has been withdrawn.

The consequences of the **wrong** use of any God-given gift cannot be blamed on God.

11 Whatever may be the mechanism of destruction before the end of the world, the final destruction will be personally inflicted by a direct act of God because the Bible says that fire will come down from God out of heaven and burn up Satan, his angels and all unrepentant sinners.

The statement in Revelation 20:9 reads, *"and fire came down from God out of heaven, and devoured them."*

To conclude that this statement means a direct and personal act of God to send fire from heaven is to ignore correct principles of exegesis or analytical interpretation.

The term "the fire of God fallen from heaven" is also found in Job 1:16 and the mechanism by which God "sent" that fire from "heaven" was the removal of His protective hedge, thus allowing the sin-perverted forces of nature to breakout into a destructive holocaust. That fire was obviously a massive storm of thunder and lightning which struck when God's restraint was removed. In fact the Today's English Version translates it as "lightning" Job 1:16 (TEV).

Now what about the final fires of Revelation. 20:9?

When the final fires "come down from God out of heaven" at the end of the millennial 1000-year reign, God will be in the Holy City New Jerusalem on earth. And no fire will come out of the Holy City. As a matter of fact the Holy City with the Godhead, the angels and all the saints will be untouched by the fire and will neither be the source nor the victim of the fiery destruction!

According to Peter and Ezekiel, the fire will have three sources. Fire from the skies (called heaven); fire from within the earth; and fire from within Satan.

Not only will God's protection and restraint be withdrawn, His life sustaining grace will also be withdrawn.

That will be the ultimate and total separation from God which sin, whenever it is finished, causes and it will produce the irreversible destruction of sinners in the second death.

> "Whereby the world that then was, being overflowed with water, perished: But the heavens and the earth, which are now, by the same word are kept in store, reserved unto fire against the day of judgment and perdition of ungodly men... But the day of the Lord will come as a thief in the night; in the which the heavens shall pass away with a great noise, and the elements shall melt with fervent heat, the earth also and the works that are therein shall be burned up. Seeing then that all these things shall be dissolved, what manner of persons ought ye to be in all holy conversation and godliness." 2 Peter 3:6,7,10,11

> "Thou hast defiled thy sanctuaries by the multitude of thine iniquities, by the iniquity of thy traffick; therefore will I bring forth a fire from the midst of thee, it shall devour thee, and I will bring thee to ashes upon the earth in the sight of all them that behold thee." Ezekiel 28:18

> "Then when lust hath conceived, it bringeth forth sin: and sin, when it is finished, bringeth forth death." James 1:15

> "For, behold, the day cometh, that shall burn as an oven; and all the proud, yea, and all that do wickedly, shall be stubble: and the day that cometh shall burn them up, saith the Lord of hosts, that it shall leave them neither root nor branch." Malachi 4:1

There are other passages in the Bible which describe the final destruction:

> *"Evil shall slay the wicked: and they that hate the righteous shall be desolate."* Psalm 34:21

> *"And he shall bring upon them their own iniquity, and shall cut them off in their own wickedness; yea, the Lord our God shall cut them off."* Psalm 94:23

> *"But he that sinneth against me wrongeth his own soul: all they that hate me love death."* Proverbs 8:36

By rejecting the righteousness of God in Christ, the unsaved will cut themselves off from God Who is the only Source of Life (See also chapter 21).

Seventeen

The Royal Law Of Liberty

God is absolutely, immutably, eternally and infinitely righteous! The moral law of God is a description of His righteousness. In other words the moral law of God is a transcript of His character, an unerring account of how God behaves in any and every circumstance.

> *"The Lord is righteous in all his ways, and holy in all his works." Psalm 145:17*

> *"For I am the Lord, I change not; therefore ye sons of Jacob are not consumed." Malachi 3:6*

> *"Every good gift and every perfect gift is from above, and cometh down from the Father of lights, with whom is no variableness, neither shadow of turning." James 1:17*

> *"Wherefore the law is holy, and the commandment holy, and just, and good." Romans 7:12*

> *"The law of the Lord is perfect, converting the soul: the testimony of the Lord is sure, making wise the simple. The statutes of the Lord are right, rejoicing the heart: the commandment of the Lord is pure, enlightening the eyes. The fear of the Lord is clean, enduring for ever: the judgments of the Lord are true and righteous altogether." Psalm 19:7-9.*

God is love. God's Agapé love is utterly unselfish, it is an "all-for-the-other" love, a love which always does the best for others whatever the cost to oneself.

"Love suffereth long, and is kind; Love envieth not; Love vaunteth not itself, is not puffed up, Doth not behave itself unseemly, seeketh not her own, is not easily provoked, thinketh no evil;" 1 Cor. 13: 4, 5

Eternal, infinite love is the fundamental functional principle of God's righteousness. Eternal, divine, Agapé love is that eternal principle within God by which He uses His eternal power righteously. This is the eternal basis of God's eternal life.

Infinite power, infinite wisdom, infinite righteousness and infinite love are all eternally inherent in God. Since love is the principle by which God unchangingly and unchangeably applies righteousness to power, we can conclude with absolute certainty that God is love, His nature, His law is love.

"He that loveth not knoweth not God; for God is love." 1 John 4:8,16.

"Love worketh no ill to his neighbour: therefore love is the fulfilling of the law." Romans 13:10.

"But whoso looketh into the perfect law of liberty, and continueth therein, he being not a forgetful hearer, but a doer of the work, this man shall be blessed in his deed." James 1:25

"If ye fulfil the royal law according to the scripture, Thou shalt love thy neighbour as thyself, ye do well:" James 2:8

Love and righteousness are therefore inseparable—in fact, righteousness is love in action. Love, the love of God, is therefore the essential functional living principle in the moral law of God. In other words, the spirit of the law is love.

"Then one of them, which was a lawyer, asked him a question, tempting him, and saying, Master, which is the great commandment in the law? Jesus said unto him, Thou shalt love the Lord thy God with all thy heart, and with all thy soul, and with all thy mind. This is the first and great commandment. And the second is like unto it, Thou shalt love thy neighbour as thyself. On these two commandments hang all the law and the prophets." Matthew 22:35-40

God's righteousness cannot be separated from His life or His love.

God cannot change His nature, He cannot change His character. To do so would be to cease from being God because since He is absolutely, eternally, infinitely perfect He cannot be improved upon neither can He deteriorate.

Therefore God cannot change His moral law which is a transcript/blueprint of His character, a description of how His nature behaves.

Similarly God **cannot** transgress or go against His nature or His character. Therefore God **cannot** transgress His moral law. Sin is defined as the transgression of God's moral law. God cannot sin, He cannot transgress His moral law. Moreover, since His moral law is perfect, God never has to break His law in order to achieve any objective. An absolute eternal and perfect law can stand on its own and can never be defeated. God's absolute moral law is not arbitrary and has no imperfections. Therefore, like His nature, it cannot be improved upon neither can its standard be lowered in anyway. No one, not even God, can change His moral law because no one, not even God, can change God's nature.

> "Think not that I am come to destroy the law, or the prophets: I am not come to destroy, but to fulfil. For verily I say unto you, Till heaven and earth pass, one jot or one tittle shall in no wise pass from the law, till all be fulfilled. Whosoever therefore shall break one of these least commandments, and shall teach men so, he shall be called the least in the kingdom of heaven: but whosoever shall do and teach them, the same shall be called great in the kingdom of heaven." Matthew 5:17-19

> "If ye keep my commandments, ye shall abide in my love; even as I have kept my Father's commandments, and abide in his love." John 15:10

> "Jesus Christ the same yesterday, and to day, and for ever." Hebrews 13:8

> "And also the Strength of Israel will not lie nor repent: for he is not a man, that he should repent." 1 Sam 15:29

Remember, we are describing God's moral law. We are not talking about the laws of creation which God made. The moral law is as eternal as God's nature, its principles are absolute and immutable. The moral law is an unerring description of God's immutable behaviour under all circumstances, to friend or foe and at all times.

The assertion that God is above His moral law, is not bound by it, and can break it, is a false assertion based on ignorance of God. It is an argument usually employed, as a desperate last resort, by those who want to avoid the claims of one or more of the Ten Commandments.

Before the development of sin, all of God's creatures possessed His law of love written in their minds and they willingly, naturally and joyfully obeyed that law of love spontaneously.

God's law of unselfish, self-sacrificing, all-for-the-other (agapé) love is the great principle which is the law of life for the universe. Since God is infinite in power, wisdom, righteousness, life and love, He is the Source of all life and of all good and it is impossible for Him to be the source of evil or death.

> *"In the way of righteousness is life; and in the pathway thereof there is no death." Proverbs 12:28*

In heaven, in His ministry for all created beings, the Son of God is the channel of all good from His Father. The Father's life, love, righteousness and blessings flow out to all through His Son and through the Son the love returns in praise and joyous service. This is the circuit of beneficence, the law of love and life for the universe.

In heaven itself this law of love and life was broken. Sin originated in self-centredness. Lucifer, the covering cherub, desired to be first in heaven. He suggested that he had a better way of governing the universe than God's way of self-sacrificing love. But there can be no other way of life than God's way, therefore Satan's government of selfishness and sin became the government of death. Satan was a liar and a murderer from the outset of his rebellion because his government would separate creatures from God's government and therefore and thereby destroy them.

> *"Whosoever committeth sin transgresseth also the law: for sin is the transgression of the law... He that committeth sin is of the devil; for the devil sinneth from the beginning. For this purpose the Son of God was manifested, that he might destroy the works of the devil." 1 John 3:4, 8*

> *"Ye are of your father the devil, and the lusts of your father ye will do. He was a murderer from the beginning, and abode not in the truth, because there is no truth in him. When he speaketh a lie, he speaketh of his own: for he is a liar, and the father of it." John 8:44.*

One third of the angelic hosts sided with Satan and the rival government was on its way. After they left heaven, Satan and his fallen angels aimed their attack on the first two humans on planet earth.

Satan's aim was to obliterate the law of love from Adam's mind and to replace it with the law of selfishness which is the law of sin and death.

He succeeded in getting Adam to disobey God and the night of woe settled down on our planet.

Mankind progressively lost the details of the principle of Divine Love from their minds until it became necessary for God to spell out those details. On Mount Sinai God spoke and wrote the Ten Commandments moral law for Israel and for the entire world (Read Exodus 20).

Scripture describes the Ten Commandment moral law as the perfect law of liberty, the royal law. This law is a complete unit describing the details of the principle of divine self-sacrificing love. In other words, the Ten Commandment moral law is God's law of love expressed in simple, unmistakable moral instructions so that every person can understand how Divine Love behaves. Moreover, this law of love expressed in the Ten Commandments is the standard for all moral judgement.

> *"But whoso looketh into the perfect law of liberty, and continueth therein, he being not a forgetful hearer, but a doer of the work, this man shall be blessed in his deed." James 1:25*

> *"If ye fulfil the royal law according to the scripture, Thou shalt love thy neighbour as thyself, ye do well: But if ye have respect to persons, ye commit sin, and are convinced of the law as transgressors. For whosoever shall keep the whole law, and yet offend in one point, he is guilty of all. For he that said, Do not commit adultery, said also, Do not kill. Now if thou commit no adultery, yet if thou kill, thou art become a transgressor of the law. So speak ye, and so do, as they that shall be judged by the law of liberty." James 2:8-12*

Since the fundamental, eternal principle in the moral law of the Ten Commandments is the principle of unselfish, self-sacrificing love, the transgression of any one commandment is the transgression of the basic principle of love which runs through each and every commandment. Therefore, to break one commandment is to break all. The love of God keeps the commandments of God.

> *"By this we know that we love the children of God, when we love God, and keep his commandments. For this is the love of God, that we keep his commandments: and his commandments are not grievous." 1 John 5:2,3*

> *"And now I beseech thee, lady, not as though I wrote a new commandment unto thee, but that which we had from the beginning, that we love one another. And this is love, that we walk after his commandments. This is the commandment, That, as ye have heard from the beginning, ye should walk in it." 2 John verse 5, 6.*

Any attempt to keep the Ten Commandments without the love of God in the soul is miserable legalism because it cannot be done. During His earthly ministry Jesus firmly and lovingly exposed the futility and emptiness of merely legal or ceremonial obedience.

We have already established that God's moral law is a **perfect** law, it is not an arbitrary set of rules but rather it is an **absolute** law based upon the eternal principle of unselfish Divine love. Therefore God never breaks His law in order to enforce it. The moral law of love, the Royal law of liberty, describes how the Divine Nature behaves under any and all circumstances.

Since the moral law is a transcript of God's character, we should be able to clearly see that God does not—in fact, cannot—break His law of love.

The moral law says, "Thou shalt not lie." God cannot lie.

> *"In hope of eternal life, which God, that cannot lie, promised before the world began;" Titus 1:2*

The moral law says, "Thou shalt not steal." God is the Giver of all good gifts and He never changes. He is not a thief, He cannot steal.

> *"Every good gift and every perfect gift is from above, and cometh down from the Father of lights, with whom is no variableness, neither shadow of turning." James 1:17*

> *"The thief cometh not, but for to steal, and to kill, and to destroy: I am come that they might have life, and that they might have it more abundantly." John 10:10*

The moral law says, "Thou shalt not kill." God is the eternal absolute Source of life He cannot be the Source of death. Those who depart from Him write off themselves. Since the moral law is a transcript of God's character, if killing is not in the law it cannot be in God's character either.

> *"Love worketh no ill to his neighbour: therefore love is the fulfilling of the law." Romans 13:10*

> *"O Lord, the hope of Israel, all that forsake thee shall be ashamed, and they that depart from me shall be written in the earth, because they have forsaken the Lord, the fountain of living waters." Jeremiah 17:13*

Sin is the cause of death. Death is inherent in sin, sin produces death as mammary glands produce milk. A farmer does not have to inject milk into the mammary glands and then milk them to get milk. **Thus it is with sin and death.**

> *"Every good gift and every perfect gift is from above, and cometh down from the Father of lights, with whom is no variableness, neither shadow of turning." James 1:17*

> *"Wherefore, as by one man sin entered into the world, and death by sin; and so death passed upon all men, for that all have sinned:" Romans 5:12*

> *"See, I have set before thee this day life and good, and death and evil; In that I command thee this day to love the Lord thy God, to walk in his ways, and to keep his commandments and his statutes and his judgments, that thou mayest live and multiply: and the Lord thy God shall bless thee in the land whither thou goest to possess it. But if thine heart turn away, so that thou wilt not hear, but shalt be drawn away, and worship other gods, and serve them;*

> *"I denounce unto you this day, that ye shall surely perish, and that ye shall not prolong your days upon the land, whither thou passest over Jordan to go to possess it. I call heaven and earth to record this day against you, that I have set before you life and death, blessing and cursing: therefore choose life, that both thou and thy seed may live:*

> *"That thou mayest love the Lord thy God, and that thou mayest obey his voice, and that thou mayest cleave unto him: for he is thy life, and the length of thy days: that thou mayest dwell in the land which the Lord sware unto thy fathers, to Abraham, to Isaac, and to Jacob, to give them." Deut 30: 15-20*

In the years leading up to the first advent of Christ the Jews had progressively lost sight of God's love in His law. They held to the "letter" of the law but, generally speaking, had rejected the principle of self-sacrificing love which is the "spirit" of the moral law. They invented a multiplicity of rules in an attempt to make themselves obedient to the moral law while all the time they were devoid of God's love.

Jesus came to show them that only by receiving the love of God in their hearts could they truly be obedient to His law.

The entire life of Jesus on earth was the perfect example of a life of love and love-motivated obedience. His life was the clearest demonstration of God's character of self-sacrificing love ever given to mankind.

"As the Father hath loved me, so have I loved you: continue ye in my love. If ye keep my commandments, ye shall abide in my love; even as I have kept my Father's commandments, and abide in his love. These things have I spoken unto you, that my joy might remain in you, and that your joy might be full. This is my commandment, That ye love one another, as I have loved you. Greater love hath no man than this, that a man lay down his life for his friends. Ye are my friends, if ye do whatsoever I command you." John 15:9-14

"I can of mine own self do nothing: as I hear, I judge: and my judgment is just; because I seek not mine own will, but the will of the Father which hath sent me." John 5:30

The love of God had been so lost sight of by the Jews, let alone the world, that they rejected the character of Christ. They were so ignorant of the true character of God they could not recognize Him in His Son.

"I have given them thy word; and the world hath hated them, because they are not of the world, even as I am not of the world. I pray not that thou shouldest take them out of the world, but that thou shouldest keep them from the evil. They are not of the world, even as I am not of the world. Sanctify them through thy truth: thy word is truth.

O righteous Father, the world hath not known thee: but I have known thee, and these have known that thou hast sent me. And I have declared unto them thy name, and will declare it: that the love wherewith thou hast loved me may be in them, and I in them." John 17:14-17, 25, 26.

THE "ACID TEST"
The prophet Isaiah gives us the "acid test."

"To the law and to the testimony: if they speak not according to this word, it is because there is no light in them." Isaiah 8:20

The life of Christ on earth was a perfect example of how to keep the Ten Commandments and a perfect demonstration of God's character of Agapé love. His life on earth was the **testimony** or **true witness** of His Father's character. When we want to know whether a doctrine is true or not we must test it by comparing it with the moral law and the perfect life of Jesus Christ.

The traditional view of a God who kills His opponents by direct decree or by direct personal attack is neither in harmony with the moral law of God nor the life of Christ.

The moral law of God declares that killing is sin.

The life of Christ was one in which He never hurt anyone and when He was urged to destroy according to what the disciples construed to be Old Testament precedent, He rebuked them with the fact that it is the spirit of Satan, not the Spirit of God, which seeks to destroy one's opponents.

> *"But he turned, and rebuked them, and said, Ye know not what manner of spirit ye are of.* For the Son of man is not come to destroy men's lives, but to save them. And they went to another village." Luke 9:55-56 note verse 55.

THE INDIVIDUAL COMMANDMENTS

THE FIRST

Thou shalt have no other gods before me. Exodus 20:3

There is only one true, living God. A true God by definition must be self-existent and must be absolutely eternal i.e. beginningless and endless. Since there is only one true God, YAHWEH, there are no others worthy of that name because all other beings are creatures.

God the Father, His Son and Holy Spirit are one God, uncreated, eternal, perfect and infinite. To turn from the true God to any other supposed god is to turn from life to non-existence. This first commandment is an expression of God's infinite love for us because He does not want us to turn from the only Source of life to sources of death.

THE SECOND

Thou shalt not make unto thee any graven image... Exodus 20:4-6

God wants us to have the correct image of Him.

A creature can rise no higher morally than the image he has of his god. To have the wrong image of the right God is equivalent to worshipping the wrong god.

We are to form the correct picture of God by allowing scripture to interpret and explain its statements about God's behaviour. Satan had made it his business to distort the correct scriptural image of God, and so when the fullness of time had come, God sent His Son to give us the right picture, the correct image of Himself.

"God, who at sundry times and in divers manners spake in time past unto the fathers by the prophets, Hath in these last days spoken unto us by his Son, whom he hath appointed heir of all things, by whom also he made the worlds; Who being the brightness of his glory, and the express image of his person, and upholding all things by the word of his power, when he had by himself purged our sins, sat down on the right hand of the Majesty on high;" Hebrews 1:1-3

Jesus is the express image of His Father and He is the Father's clearest and fullest expression of His character, therefore all statements about God must be interpreted and explained by the demonstration given by the life, death and resurrection of Jesus Christ.

"For the law was given by Moses, but grace and truth came by Jesus Christ. No man hath seen God at any time; the only begotten Son, which is in the bosom of the Father, he hath declared him." John 1:17, 18

THE THIRD

Thou shalt not take the name of the LORD (YAHWEH) thy God in vain; for the Lord will not hold him guiltless that taketh his name in vain. Exodus 20:7.

To take God's name in vain means more than using His name irreverently or disrespectfully. It includes false profession. To profess to be a child of God, calling on His Name and using His name, while denying His claims or rejecting His righteousness is to take God's name in vain.

"Not every one that saith unto me, Lord, Lord, shall enter into the kingdom of heaven; but he that doeth the will of my Father which is in heaven. Many will say to me in that day, Lord, Lord, have we not prophesied in thy name? and in thy name have cast out devils? and in thy name done many wonderful works? And then will I profess unto them, I never knew you: depart from me, ye that work iniquity." Matthew 7:21-23.

To use the name of God while believing Satan's lies about God's character is also to take God's name in vain.

THE FOURTH

Remember the Sabbath day to keep it holy six days shalt thou labour, and do all thy work: But the seventh day is the Sabbath of the LORD

(YAHWEH) thy God: in it thou shalt not do any work, thou, nor thy son, nor thy daughters, thy manservant, nor thy maidservant, nor thy cattle, nor thy stranger that is within thy gates.

For in six days the Lord made the heaven and earth, the sea, and all that in them is, and rested the seventh-day: wherefore the Lord blessed the Sabbath day and hallowed it. Exodus 20:8-11.

God could have spoken our planet into complete perfection by one word but He chose to speak the crude planet into existence and then in six days to make it, shape it and create all that was necessary to make it a complete and perfect paradise for mankind.

Why?

By the time our planet and solar system were to be created, sin had already developed in the universe. The assertion of Satan's government was that creatures did not need God's government of righteousness. God intended to show that every detail of His creative work had to be accomplished in, by and through **complete** righteousness. Any detail of the creation not constructed in complete righteousness would mean a defect which would spell eventual ruin.

During Creation Week God proceeded, day by day, with His creative work until our planet was a **completely perfect** paradise and He pronounced it very good.

"And God saw every thing that he had made, and, behold, it was very good. And the evening and the morning were the sixth day." Genesis 1:31

"Thus the heavens and the earth were finished, and all the host of them. And on the seventh day God ended his work which he had made; and he rested on the seventh day from all his work which he had made. And God blessed the seventh day, and sanctified it: because that in it he had rested from all his work which God created and made." Genesis 2:1-3

Every detail of creation was **completely** covered and filled with righteousness. Seven is God's number of completeness. If God had stopped His creative work on the first day of the week or on any day before completion there could have been no rest because the earth would have been a long way from the completely perfect paradise He intended it to be. Rest is the end-result of righteousness.

"And the work of righteousness shall be peace; and the effect of righteousness quietness and assurance for ever." Isaiah 32:17

The seventh day Sabbath is therefore the immutable memorial and sign of the fact that God's righteousness must cover and fill His creation in order for existence and life to be perfectly maintained. The weekly seventh-day Sabbath is the constant reminder of our need to have God's righteousness completely applied to every aspect of our beings.

The righteousness of God is functionally constituted in Christ, therefore in Him we have complete righteousness and rest.

"But of him are ye in Christ Jesus, who of God is made unto us wisdom, and righteousness, and sanctification, and redemption:" 1 Cor 1:30

"Come unto me, all ye that labour and are heavy laden, and I will give you rest. Take my yoke upon you, and learn of me; for I am meek and lowly in heart: and ye shall find rest unto your souls." Matt 11:28-29

When Jesus was here on earth, He unequivocally stated that the Sabbath was made for mankind. He had to have been absolutely correct for He was the One who made all things perfect and complete in the beginning, including the Sabbath.

"And he said unto them, The sabbath was made for man, and not man for the sabbath: Therefore the Son of man is Lord also of the sabbath." Mark 2:27,28

"In the beginning was the Word, and the Word was with God, and the Word was God. The same was in the beginning with God. All things were made by him; and without him was not any thing made that was made." John 1:1-3

"There remaineth therefore a rest to the people of God. For he that is entered into his rest, he also hath ceased from his own works, as God did from his.

For he spake in a certain place of the seventh day on this wise, And God did rest the seventh day from all his works." Hebrews 4:9, 10,4

It is clear then that since the weekly seventh-day Sabbath was established before the entrance of sin in the earth, it is not and can never be a shadow or ceremony but rather a constant reminder of the facts that:

(i)   God is the Creator and

(ii) The creation needs to be completely detailed with God's righteousness in order for things to work perfectly right.

Therefore the command to remember the Sabbath Day to keep it holy is of the highest moral order. It is in fact the most moral of all the Ten Commandments and it is the commandment which binds or seals the Ten Commandments into one moral unit of love. And all this because the seventh-day Sabbath teaches, as no other command does, that creation must have God's complete righteousness and that only the Creator God can give that righteousness and apply it to every detail with absolute completeness, hence the number 7.

God knew that to forget the Sabbath would be to forget the very basis of all morality which is the righteousness of God given and applied to us by the Creator. So it is not any one day in seven, it is only the seventh-day of the week which can be the reminder of the Creator's creative righteousness. No other day can be the Sabbath but the seventh-day of the week.

Furthermore, in remembering the seventh-day Sabbath, to keep it holy, there is the highest state and sense of freedom because it is the righteousness of God that liberates from bondage to sin.

Love for God manifests itself in loving obedience to the first four commandments. We come now to the last six commandments, which describe the details of how love behaves towards others.

THE FIFTH

Honor thy father and thy mother that thy days may be long upon the land which the Lord thy God giveth thee. Exodus 20:12

God made the family unit. Human children need loving instruction and guidance throughout the first three seven-year periods of their life, i.e. up to age 21. Children should love, honor, respect and submit to righteous parental authority. And parents should ensure that their authority is that of love and righteousness.

THE SIXTH

Thou shalt not kill. Exodus 20:13.

God is the only Source of created life. And He is not the Source of death. Death came as a result of sin, and were it not for the redemption of Christ, death would have been permanent. Because of Christ's redemptive work, physical death is called (i) a sleep and (ii) the first death, by implication, since there is a second death.

God is the Giver of all good gifts. He neither changes nor varies, He is never the giver of bad gifts and death is so bad it is called an enemy of God and God is never the Source of anything inimical to Himself.

"Every good gift and every perfect gift is from above, and cometh down from the Father of lights, with whom is no variableness, neither shadow of turning. Of his own will begat he us with the word of truth, that we should be a kind of firstfruits of his creatures. Wherefore, my beloved brethren, let every man be swift to hear, slow to speak, slow to wrath: For the wrath of man worketh not the righteousness of God." James 1:17-20

"Then cometh the end, when he shall have delivered up the kingdom to God, even the Father; when he shall have put down all rule and all authority and power. For he must reign, till he hath put all enemies under his feet. The last enemy that shall be destroyed is death." 1 Cor. 15:24-26

Death is the enemy of God and His creation and He intends to destroy it. He is not the cause of it. To inflict death on anyone, to kill anyone is the lowest level of morality, it is using the enemy of God against the Creator's creatures. God values life so very highly that He is hurt even when a sparrow falls dead to the ground!

When we have God's love in our souls we will value life as highly as God does. God kills no one; neither should we. Rather, we should seek to promote health and save life.

Sickness, suffering and death are the result of the sin-problem on earth. God is the One Who restores. Satan, with his government of sin, is the destroyer.

"The thief cometh not, but for to steal, and to kill, and to destroy: I am come that they might have life, and that they might have it more abundantly." John 10:10

"Bless the Lord, O my soul: and all that is within me, bless his holy name. Bless the Lord, O my soul, and forget not all his benefits: Who forgiveth all thine iniquities; who healeth all thy diseases; Who redeemeth thy life from destruction; who crowneth thee with lovingkindness and tender mercies; Who satisfieth thy mouth with good things; so that thy youth is renewed like the eagle's." Psalm 103:1-5.

THE SEVENTH

Thou shalt not commit adultery. Exodus 20:14

In Ephesians 5 Paul teaches us that physical marriage is a symbol of the marriage between Christ and His church. One of the most strikingly lovely characteristics of the Divine Nature is God's faithfulness, His loyalty, His commitment to His creatures through His selfless love.

Marriage was ordained for the reproduction of the race and to provide an environment of love, faithfulness, loyalty and commitment for human family life.

To every natural power or biological system which He made God fixed particular and specific principles of righteousness. To transgress these principles is to expose the particular natural power or system to perversion of function with resultant physical, mental and spiritual disaster.

Sexual immorality exposes the biological systems involved to the damage which always results when sin separates any aspect of creation from God's righteousness.

> *"Flee fornication. Every sin that a man doeth is without the body; but he that committeth fornication sinneth against his own body. What? know ye not that your body is the temple of the Holy Ghost which is in you, which ye have of God, and ye are not your own? For ye are bought with a price: therefore glorify God in your body, and in your spirit, which are God's."* 1 Cor. 6:18-20.

THE EIGHTH

Thou shalt not steal. Exodus 20:15.

Agapé Love always gives. Love does not even seek its own let alone what belongs to others.

The love of God always moves its possessor to give, to share, not looking for anything in return. Our Heavenly Father has set us the example.

> *"God so loved the world, that He gave His only begotten Son."*

THE NINTH

Thou shalt not bear false witness against thy neighbour. Exodus 20:16.

A lie or falsehood describes that which is not. All lies therefore contain the seeds of non-existence or death masquerading under the guise of existence. To believe a lie or to tell a lie is to be a purveyor of death.

THE TENTH

Thou shalt not covet ... Exodus 20:17.

Covetousness is idolatry. It is a cardinal manifestation of selfishness which is the opposite of God's self-sacrificing, "all-for-the-other", love.

Covetousness is the springboard of theft. Rather than seeking others' possessions we should follow the counsel of Jesus in Matthew 6:33, 34.

> *"But seek ye first the kingdom of God, and his righteousness; and all these things shall be added unto you. Take therefore no thought for the morrow: for the morrow shall take thought for the things of itself. Sufficient unto the day is the evil thereof." Matthew 6:33, 34.*

Conclusion

There is not a commandment of the law that is not for the good and happiness of man, both in this life and in the life to come. In obedience to God's law, man is surrounded as with a hedge and kept from evil. Anyone who breaks down this divinely erected barrier at one point has destroyed its power to protect him, for he has opened a way by which the enemy can enter to waste and ruin.

The absolute moral law of Agapé love in the ten commandments, as well as the gospel, reflects the true character of God.

> *"In the way of righteousness is life; and in the pathway thereof is no death." Proverbs 12:28.*

Since there is no death in the way of righteousness God can never be the Source of death because He is absolutely, eternally, infinitely righteous and immutably so.

The sting of death is sin (1 Cor 15:56).

The wages of sin is death. (Romans 6:23).

The law can be kept only by abiding in Christ and having His love, faith and righteousness in our hearts.

Eighteen

The Character Of God And
The Plan Of Redemption

God did not ordain that sin should develop in His creation but He foresaw, from all eternity past, its development in Lucifer's mind, its spread to other angels and ultimately to humans on planet earth. From all eternity past, God the Father and His Son, through their eternal **Spirit of love** had agreed on the plan of redemption. This was put into effect the minute Adam disobeyed and "sold out" our entire world to Satan's government.

From the instant Adam sinned, our entire planet was **separated** from God's perfect life-giving government of love and righteousness but the Son of God immediately **stood** in the **gap** which sin had made. God's grace enabled **corporate humanity** to survive by holding in check the forces of evil while sustaining existence and life on the rebellious planet.

Because the Son of God had made His commitment from all eternity past and then actually stood in the **gap of separation** after Adam's fall, He is described as the Lamb slain from the foundation of the world! (Rev.13:8).

At last when the fullness of time had come, the eternal Son of God entered our time, our nature and our world as a human being; the Second Person of the Godhead had become incarnate, the Son of God became the Son of man.

> *"Who hath saved us, and called us with an holy calling, not according to our works, but according to his own purpose and grace, which was given us in Christ Jesus before the world began, But is now made manifest by the appearing of our Saviour Jesus Christ, who hath abolished death, and hath brought life and immortality to light through the gospel:"*
> *2 Tim. 1:9, 10*

> *"But we speak the wisdom of God in a mystery, even the hidden wisdom, which God ordained before the world unto our glory:" 1 Cor. 2:7*

"Now to him that is of power to stablish you according to my gospel, and the preaching of Jesus Christ, according to the revelation of the mystery, which was kept secret since the world began," Romans 16:25

Between the fall of mankind in Adam and the incarnation of the Son of God, the human race was given the Old Testament system of animal sacrifices which was eventually systematized into the ceremonies and services of the earthly sanctuary or earthly temple. Each time the sinner killed a lamb, or other animal, he was to be taught the terrible truth that it is sin which causes death. And more importantly, he was to be taught the amazing, the fantastic, the incredibly good news that the Son of God would come to earth to be killed by our sins in order to redeem or buy back all that was sold out by Adam's one act of disobedience!

"Therefore as by the offence of one judgment came upon all men to condemnation; even so by the righteousness of one the free gift came upon all men unto justification of life." Romans 5:18

Satan understood, to some extent, the meaning of the sacrificial sanctuary services and he worked diligently to pervert the Jewish understanding of the significance of those services. He succeeded to a considerable extent in causing the people to picture God as a cruel tyrant who delighted in the death of countless animals. And so the Jews saw the sacrifices as necessary to appease God's wrath and earn His favour rather than seeing them as promises of love which pointed forward to God's love-gift of His only begotten Son to save the lost race of Adam.

Going back now into eternity past we see that the Son of God pledged Himself in covenant with His Father to be the Substitute and Surety, the Second Adam, the Saviour for the whole world.

And just as God had foreseen **lost** humanity in the **first** Adam, He foresaw **redeemed** humanity in the **Second** Adam, Jesus Christ!

*"**Blessed be the God and Father of our Lord Jesus Christ, who hath blessed us with all spiritual blessings in heavenly places in Christ:**... According as he hath chosen us in him before the foundation of the world, that we should be holy and without blame before him in love: Having predestinated us unto the adoption of children by Jesus Christ to himself, according to the good pleasure of his will, To the praise of the glory of his grace, wherein he hath made us accepted in the beloved." Ephesians 1:3, 4-6.*

First, The Bad News

In order to better appreciate God's amazing plan of redemption we need to understand, a little better than we usually do, the extent of what we lost in the fall of Adam.

Before the Fall, Adam possessed sinless, unfallen human flesh i.e sinless physical human nature, which was most conducive to submissive obedience. He also possessed a sinless, innocent, unfallen human character, which would have grown into sinless maturity by obedience to God. The Holy Spirit of the Father and Son indwelt the spirit of Adam's mind and all his thoughts were governed by and filled with God's self-sacrificing Agapé love.

The world was perfect. There was no sin, no decay, and no death. In fact, before sin entered our world, nothing could have gone wrong because God's perfect Government of Glory was in full and absolute control of our world and our universe.

The Extent Of Sin's Damage To Man

When Adam sinned, he expelled the Agapé love of God in the Holy Spirit from his mind and lost his innocent character. His human body was separated from God's government and subsequently his flesh became fallen, sinful flesh, no longer conducive to submissive obedience.

Adam was, in fact, Representative Man. He represented the whole race. The whole race was in him when he sinned and his choice to sin was representative choice.

Adam's one act of disobedience "wrote off" human character and human nature. He sold out the entire race and the entire planet to Satan's government of sin. At that moment when Adam disobeyed God, corporate humanity disobeyed in him and all was lost.

Adam's human nature before the fall was physically perfect, structurally and functionally unfallen. Adam's brain functions, the biochemistry of the thinking process and his mental faculties were also perfect.

After the fall, human nature also developed physical infirmities. No longer did the physical human nature function with the unfallen perfection as before the entrance of sin. The mental faculties also became weakened.

But the most damaging of the infirmities of the flesh which developed progressively after the fall was its moral infirmity. What do we mean by moral infirmity? We mean that the fallen physical human nature, far from being conducive to submissive obedience, became antagonistic to submissive obedience. The fallen flesh would exert a pull on the mind, a pull away from God's love and righteousness.

Satan recognized the extent of the stranglehold he had on the race. He exulted that he had seduced Adam to sin in sinless nature and he thought that now that Adam's nature was fallen he would forever hold the human race in his grasp.

But what Satan did not bargain for was the extent to which God's unselfish love would go to rescue man!

What Would Be Required To Redeem Man

Since the sin problem could only be overcome by love and right, rather than by power and might, God faced a massive problem. The sin problem would be the severest test His government would have to face.

If it were a matter of force or power it would have been an easy and very quick work for God to overcome Satan's government, as easy and quick as speaking the word since God does everything by His word.

But it is a matter of right **not** might!

God's government would have to overcome all the cruelty, all the hatred, all the force, all the lies and deception that Satan's government could produce. And God's government would have to overcome not by force but by the power of love and righteousness!

The question that therefore naturally arose in the minds of the on-looking universe was: Could God's harmless love be victorious over Satan's violent and cruel selfishness? The principles of God's government would be put to the severest test by the sin problem.

The challenge was infinitely immense! God could not shrink from it. He would meet it through the incarnation, earthly life, death, resurrection and heavenly ministration of His Son!

In order to destroy the works of the devil without force, the Son of God, Eternal Wisdom, (Proverbs 8) would have to apply God's righteousness by His love to whatever extent sin had produced its damage.

Because sin separated man from God, the Son of God would have to suffer the death which the ultimate separation from God causes.

And because the law of sin and death became entrenched in fallen human flesh, the Son of God would have to take on our fallen flesh and conquer the law of sin and death resident in such flesh.

In order to buy back or redeem Adam's lost race, the Son of God would have to live a sinless life in our fallen sinful flesh and die the equivalent of the death, which Adam would have died, if there were no plan of redemption. The Son of God would have to go to the lowest depths to apply righteousness by love in order to reconcile humanity to God.

Such was the magnitude of the problem that laid outstretched before Him before He left Heaven to come to earth in His first Advent.

The Fullness Of Time

"But when the fulness of the time was come, God sent forth his Son, made of a woman, made under the law, To redeem them that were under the law, that we might receive the adoption of sons." Galatians 4:4,5.

"Christ hath redeemed us from the curse of the law, being made a curse for us: for it is written, Cursed is every one that hangeth on a tree:" Galatians 3:13

Some four thousand years after the fall, when sin's damage to fallen human nature was at a critically high level, the Son of God became incarnate. He was made of a woman and made under the law, the meaning of which Paul gives in 2 Cor. 5:21.

"For he hath made him to be sin for us, who knew no sin; that we might be made the righteousness of God in him." 2 Cor. 5:21.

Though He never committed a sin in His life, yet by taking on our fallen heredity He therefore and thereby took on our condemnation.

The "Word" Became Flesh

"In the beginning was the Word, and the Word was with God, and the Word was God... And the Word was made flesh, and dwelt among us, (and we beheld his glory, the glory as of the only begotten of the Father,) full of grace and truth." John 1:1, 14.

The Son of God is called the **WORD**, (Greek: Logos) in John 1:1. In Proverbs chapter 8 He is called the **WISDOM** of God.

The eternal Wisdom of God, the WORD, the "logos," the eternal Son of God became flesh.

"Let this mind be in you, which was also in Christ Jesus: Who, being in the form of God, thought it not robbery to be equal with God: But made himself of no reputation, and took upon him the form of a servant, and was made in the likeness of men:" Philippians 2:5-7.

In Philippians 2:5-7 Paul explains that Christ Jesus, who was in the form and nature of God, humbled Himself and took upon Himself the form and nature of man.

Similarly, in Hebrews 1, Paul explains that the Son of God in Heaven was higher than any angel because He, (like His Father), was God in nature from eternity, whereas the angels are created beings. Then in Hebrews 2, Paul proceeds to explain that the Son of God took on human nature in order to save mankind from sin. He who was God in nature, became man. The Word was made flesh.

What Kind Of Flesh?

The question may be asked: What kind of human nature, what kind of flesh did the Son of God take upon himself when He became man? This question is critically important. The answer is so clearly stated in the Bible that no one needs to be mistaken.

The following texts clearly prove that the Son of God took upon Himself our **sinful flesh**, overcame that flesh and lived a **sinless life** in perfect obedience to the WILL OF GOD.

> *"Concerning his Son Jesus Christ our Lord, which was made of the seed of David according to the flesh;" Romans 1:3*

> *"For what the law could not do, in that it was weak through the flesh, God sending his own Son in the likeness of sinful flesh, and for sin, condemned sin in the flesh:" Romans 8:3*

> *"Forasmuch then as the children are partakers of flesh and blood, he also himself likewise took part of the same; that through death he might destroy him that had the power of death, that is, the devil; And deliver them who through fear of death were all their lifetime subject to bondage. For verily he took not on him the nature of angels; but he took on him the seed of Abraham. Wherefore in all things it behoved him to be made like unto his brethren, that he might be a merciful and faithful high priest in things pertaining to God, to make reconciliation for the sins of the people. For in that he himself hath suffered being tempted, he is able to succour them that are tempted." Hebrews 2:14-18*

> *"And the Word was made flesh, and dwelt among us, (and we beheld his glory, the glory as of the only begotten of the Father,) full of grace and truth." John 1:14*

> *"And without controversy great is the mystery of godliness: God was manifest in the flesh, justified in the Spirit, seen of angels, preached unto the Gentiles, believed on in the world, received up into glory." 1 Tim. 3:16*

"Beloved, believe not every spirit, but try the spirits whether they are of God: because many false prophets are gone out into the world. Hereby know ye the Spirit of God: Every spirit that confesseth that Jesus Christ is come in the flesh is of God: And every spirit that confesseth not that Jesus Christ is come in the flesh is not of God: and this is that spirit of antichrist, whereof ye have heard that it should come; and even now already is it in the world." 1 John 4:1-3

Let us carefully examine the first three texts:

(i)   Romans 1:3 *"Concerning His Son Jesus Christ our Lord, who was made of the seed of David according to the flesh."*
This text clearly teaches that the kind of human flesh Jesus had was the same kind as that of the seed of David and was made of the seed of David. Such flesh obviously was not the same flesh that Adam had before his fall. The flesh of the seed of David was sinful fallen flesh.

(ii) Romans 8:3 *"For what the law could not do, in that it was weak through the flesh, God sending His own Son in the likeness of sinful flesh, and for sin, condemned sin in the flesh."*
The Greek word translated **likeness** in this text is the same word used in Philippians 2:7. It really means **same** or **actual**. What Paul is saying in Romans 8:3,4 is that Jesus came in the same weak sinful flesh which we have **but He overcame that flesh for us** so that, by faith in Him, we too may live righteous lives in spite of our sinful flesh!

(iii) Hebrews 2:14 *"Forasmuch then as the children are partakers of flesh and blood, He also himself likewise took part of the same; that through death He might destroy him that had the power of death, that is, the devil."*
This text plainly teaches that Jesus partook of the **same** flesh and blood as those He came to save, that is, sinful flesh. Verse 16 emphasizes the fact that He took on Himself not the nature of angels but the nature of Abraham's seed. The nature of Abraham's seed was certainly not the nature of unfallen Adam, it was sinful, fallen flesh!

Some people equate sinful flesh with sinful character. This is a terrible mistake. We commit sin when we allow the flesh to control the mind. Jesus never gave in to the flesh. He lived a sinless character in our sinful flesh and it is because of this blessed fact that we glory in the tremendous victory of Jesus Christ.

He Was Tempted In All Points As We Are Tempted
The Apostle Paul wrote down an amazing truth in Hebrews 4:15.

*"For we have not an high priest who cannot be touched with the feelings of our infirmities; **but was in all points tempted like as we are, yet without sin.**"*

Jesus Christ was **tempted in all points** just like us. But in order to be tempted in all points like us, **he had to be made in all things like us**!

"Wherefore in all things it behoved Him to be made like unto His brethren, that He might be a merciful and faithful high priest in things pertaining to God, to make reconciliation for the sins of the people." Hebrews 2:17.

By putting the two texts together (Hebrews 4:15 and Hebrews 2:17 we can understand clearly Paul's argument. He is saying that in order for Jesus to qualify as a merciful high priest He had to be tempted in all points just like we are. But in order for Him to be tempted in all points like us, He had to be made in all things like us **therefore he had to take upon himself our sinful flesh which is one of our main sources of temptation!**

It is crucially important to understand that Christ could not have been tempted in all points like us if He had not taken on our sinful flesh!

Yes friend, Jesus was tempted in all points like you are. He fully understands the trials and temptations of the fallen flesh, the enticing attractions of the sinful world and the direct attacks of Satan. In our weak, sinful flesh, Jesus endured every enticing temptation to sin which we have to face. Therefore He knows how to sympathize with us and how to help us. As a matter of fact He was tempted beyond the point of human endurance. In the Garden of Gethsemane and in His trial and crucifixion, He was tortured and abused while at the same time He was bearing the sins and guilt of the entire world!

Throughout His entire life, especially in His last 24 hours, He was tempted not only to break God's commandments but also to save Himself, to defend Himself, to retaliate against His enemies, to give up in the great struggle against sin. But He overcame each and every temptation.

Dear reader, it is because of His victory that we too can overcome. He overcame the sinful flesh in order that we too may be able to overcome the sinful flesh. Read Hebrews 2:14-18 again and thank God for the wonderful gift of victory given to us in Christ! Read also Hebrews 12:1-3.

Since Jesus was tempted in all points like us, and since He felt all the enticements of the sinful flesh and moreover, since He overcame and lived a spotlessly sinless life, **then we have the assurance of victory by faith in him.**

"There hath no temptation taken you but such as is common to man: but God is faithful who will not suffer you to be tempted above what ye are able; but will with the temptation also make a way of escape, that ye may be able to bear it." 1 Corinthians 10:13.

But the question may be asked: How did Jesus overcome the flesh, the world and the devil?

Jesus Overcame By Faith In, And Absolute Surrender To, His Father

Many people believe that Jesus overcame by depending on His own strength. Many feel that He overcame because His human flesh was superior to ours.

We have seen clearly from the Bible that He had the same weak sinful flesh we have. The Bible also makes it clear that Jesus did not employ His own Divinity in the fight against sin.

Jesus Christ overcame not by depending on His own Godhood, but by absolute surrender to His Father in full faith. Consider carefully these texts where Jesus explains that He trusted and depended completely upon His Father to do the works of righteousness through Him.

__"I can of my own self do nothing;__ as I hear I judge; and my judgment is just; because __I seek not mine own will but the will of the Father which hath sent me."__ John 5:30.

"For I came down from heaven, not to do mine own will, but the will of Him that sent me." John 6:38.

"Verily, verily, I say unto you, __The Son can do nothing__ of Himself but what he seeth the Father do: for what things soever he doeth, these also doeth the Son likewise." John 5:19.

"Believest thou not that I am in the Father, and the Father in Me? The words that I speak unto you __I speak not of Myself: but the Father that dwelleth in me, He doeth the works."__ John 14:10.

"For even Christ pleased not himself; but, as it is written, The reproaches of them that reproached thee fell on me." Romans 15:3

"And he went a little farther, and fell on his face, and prayed, saying, O my Father, if it be possible, let this cup pass from me: nevertheless not as I will, but as thou wilt." Matthew 26:39

When Jesus Christ was on earth in human nature He depended not on himself but upon His Heavenly Father. He entrusted His entire life to the Heavenly Father who by the Holy Spirit performed the works of righteousness through the Son.

Jesus had to pray and cry out to the Father to keep him from falling under the attacks of the enemy. Paul makes this clear in Hebrews 5:7-9.

> *"Who in the days of his flesh, when he had offered up prayers and supplications with strong crying and tears unto him that was able to save him from death, and was heard in that he feared; Though he were a Son, yet learned he obedience by the things which he suffered; And being made perfect, he became the author of eternal salvation unto all them that obey him;" Hebrews 5:7-9.*

The righteousness of Christ then was righteousness by faith in God and not by self-effort. By faith in God He surrendered all to His Father who produced the good works of righteousness in and through Him.

The faith of Jesus is therefore the victorious faith of absolute surrender to God, of absolute trust in God, of absolute dependence on God, of absolute belief in God's word to be the substance of things hoped for and the evidence of things not seen.

The faith of Jesus is the faith of victory over sin, over the flesh, over the world and over Satan. The faith of Jesus produces complete obedience to the will of God, **to the Ten Commandments of God.**

The faith of Jesus allows God to fully reproduce His character through the believer in Christ!

God's final generation of living believers will keep the commandments of God because they will have the faith of Jesus, Revelation 14:12.

Remember, righteousness is not produced by our self-effort to do right. True, saving righteousness is the **righteousness of God in Christ** and is received as **a free gift** by the believing sinner. The gift of righteousness transforms the believer's character, making him obedient to the will of God. The secret, then, of how to obtain righteousness is clearly revealed by the faith of Jesus. It is the **surrender of self** to God in full faith, receiving His forgiveness, His love and His righteousness as free gifts in Christ by the Holy Spirit.

> *"... And this is the victory that overcometh the world even our faith."*
> *1 John 5:4.*

Nineteen

Is The Good News Too Good For Some To Believe?

All that was **sold out** by the disobedience of the first Adam has been **bought back** or **redeemed** by the perfect obedience and infinite sacrifice of the Second Adam, our Lord and Saviour Jesus Christ. To *redeem* means to *buy back*.

By taking on our sinful flesh and living a sinless life, and by dying the equivalent of the second death for us, Jesus has already reconciled corporate humanity to God. He has paid the redemption price for all human beings. Therefore, all human beings have been bought back or redeemed by the infinite sacrifice of Christ!

> *"Therefore as by the offence of one judgment came upon all men to condemnation; even so by the righteousness of one the free gift came upon all men unto justification of life." Romans 5:18*

> *"But we see Jesus, who was made a little lower than the angels for the suffering of death, crowned with glory and honour; that he by the grace of God should taste death for every man." Hebrews 2:9*

Just as Adam's disobedience sold out corporate humanity, i.e the whole human race, so too Christ's obedience even unto the death of the cross has bought back or redeemed corporate humanity.

God has already given the free gift of salvation to corporate humanity in Christ. Christ is the Second Adam, our New Representative Man, therefore when He died for all, all died in Him.

> *"For the love of Christ constraineth us; because we thus judge, that if one died for all, then were all dead:" 2 Cor. 5:14*

"And said unto the woman, Now we believe, not because of thy saying: for we have heard him ourselves, and know that this is indeed the Christ, the Saviour of the world." John 4:42

But God has made us all free moral agents with freedom of choice. We can choose to give ourselves fully to Jesus acknowledging that we are already His both by creation and redemption, or we can refuse to acknowledge or believe the fact that He has already paid the infinite price for our salvation and therefore refuse to give ourselves to Him.

But those who believe that Jesus has already redeemed them by His death and in heart-felt, love-motivated response surrender fully to Him, they are saved by His life, and have experienced justification by faith!

"But God commendeth his love toward us, in that, while we were yet sinners, Christ died for us. Much more then, being now justified by his blood, we shall be saved from wrath through him. For if, when we were enemies, we were reconciled to God by the death of his Son, much more, being reconciled, we shall be saved by his life." Romans 5:8-10.

"For the love of Christ constraineth us; because we thus judge, that if one died for all, then were all dead: And he died for all, that they which live should not henceforth live unto themselves, but unto him which died for them, and rose again. Wherefore henceforth know we no man after the flesh: yea, though we have known Christ after the flesh, yet now henceforth know we him no more. Therefore if any man be in Christ, he is a new creature: old things are passed away; behold, all things are become new.

And all things are of God, who hath reconciled us to himself by Jesus Christ, and hath given to us the ministry of reconciliation; To wit, that God was in Christ, reconciling the world unto himself, not imputing their trespasses unto them; and hath committed unto us the word of reconciliation. Now then we are ambassadors for Christ, as though God did beseech you by us: we pray you in Christ's stead, be ye reconciled to God. For he hath made him to be sin for us, who knew no sin; that we might be made the righteousness of God in him." 2 Cor. 5:14-21

"For therefore we both labour and suffer reproach, because we trust in the living God, who is the Saviour of all men, specially of those that believe." 1 Timothy 4:10

What amazing love! What a wonderful salvation!

The Son of God, the Second Person of the Godhead, the One Who made all men in the First Adam, the One Who stood in the gap of the separation from God caused by Adam's sin, He condescended to be born into the human race, to take on our corporate fallen human nature, to be really tempted in all points as we are, to perfectly obey God's law for us and to die for us the death which sin's separation from God causes!

> *"Let this mind be in you, which was also in Christ Jesus: Who, being in the form of God, thought it not robbery to be equal with God: But made himself of no reputation, and took upon him the form of a servant, and was made in the likeness of men: And being found in fashion as a man, he humbled himself, and became obedient unto death, even the death of the cross." Philippians 2:5-8.*

And He did all of that because of His unconditional love for mankind. God loves us not because we are worthy, not because of who we are but because of Who He is! We are worthy only because He loves us with an infinite love.

Rather than leave us to perish because of our own sins, He took all the suffering and death that Satan's government could have thrown at Him. He did this in order to set us free. In fact He was willing to be separated from His Father forever in order to save us from sin and its consequences.

> *"That whosoever believeth in him should not perish, but have eternal life. For God so loved the world, that he gave his only begotten Son, that whosoever believeth in him should not perish, but have everlasting life. For God sent not his Son into the world to condemn the world; but that the world through him might be saved." John 3:15-17.*

Adam's one act of disobedience had brought the verdict of guilt and condemnation upon corporate humanity. But Christ's obedience, even unto the death of the cross, brought the verdict of acquittal or legal justification for corporate humanity!

This is illustrated by a piece of history. In 1863 Abraham Lincoln's Emancipation Proclamation abolished slavery and legally set all American slaves free; but no slave could **experience** that freedom until he (i) heard the good news that he was **already** freed, (ii) **believed** it to be a fact, and (iii) allowed the good news of his freedom to **motivate** him to walk off the slave-plantation into a new life of liberty. If he chose to remain a slave it was because of either ignorance or rejection of the gift of liberty.

No one needs to be lost! But the vast majority of people will be lost not because Christ hasn't paid their redemptive price, not because God hasn't given the free gift of salvation to all men in Christ, but because of their unbelief and rejection of the gift of salvation.

This Good News of God's unconditional love and what He has already accomplished for us in Christ at Calvary is the Gospel. It is this love, and nothing else, that will motivate the sinner to give up all of himself to Jesus, to surrender all at the foot of the Cross in gratitude for such a sacrifice and such love!

It is only such wonderful love and goodness which can produce genuine-heart felt sorrow for sin and the motive-power to turn from sin to God in heart-broken anguish for our sins; sins which killed God's only Son.

Only the love of God revealed at Calvary can motivate self-centred humans to overcome selfishness and live unselfishly for God by receiving the free gift of righteousness. We can now read the following texts joyfully:

> *"Or despisest thou the riches of his goodness and forbearance and longsuffering; not knowing that the goodness of God leadeth thee to repentance?" Romans 2:4*

> *"And we have known and believed the love that God hath to us. God is love; and he that dwelleth in love dwelleth in God, and God in him. Herein is our love made perfect, that we may have boldness in the day of judgment: because as he is, so are we in this world. There is no fear in love; but perfect love casteth out fear: because fear hath torment. He that feareth is not made perfect in love. We love him, because he first loved us." 1 John 4:16-19*

> *"That he would grant you, according to the riches of his glory, to be strengthened with might by his Spirit in the inner man; That Christ may dwell in your hearts by faith; that ye, being rooted and grounded in love, May be able to comprehend with all saints what is the breadth, and length, and depth, and height; And to know the love of Christ, which passeth knowledge, that ye might be filled with all the fulness of God. Now unto him that is able to do exceeding abundantly above all that we ask or think, according to the power that worketh in us," Ephesians 3:16-20*

Grace Is Stronger Than Sin

Moreover, God has made it easier to be saved than to be lost. God's infinite, unconditional love has given to corporate humanity the infinite gift of salvation from sin. This love of God in the Holy Spirit invites, pleads with and draws the sinner to Christ. If the sinner resists and beats back the wooing mercy of God's love, the Spirit intensifies His convicting and convincing work on the soul. For one to be lost he has to persistently beat back all the drawing power of God's Spirit of love, but if he yields himself to the drawing of the Holy Spirit he will completely surrender self to Jesus Christ to receive and therefore to experience the gift of righteousness and eternal life.

> *"Moreover, the law entered, that the offence might abound. But where sin abounded, grace did much more abound: That as sin hath reigned unto death, even so might grace reign through righteousness unto eternal life by Jesus Christ our Lord." Romans 5:20, 21*

> *"The Lord hath appeared of old unto me, saying, Yea, I have loved thee with an everlasting love: therefore with lovingkindness have I drawn thee." Jeremiah 31:3*

The Faith Response

God loves and gives; our part is to believe, surrender and receive.

> *"For God so loved the world, that he gave his only begotten Son, that whosoever believeth in him should not perish, but have everlasting life." John 3:16*

> *"But as many as received him, to them gave he power to become the sons of God, even to them that believe on his name: Which were born, not of blood, nor of the will of the flesh, nor of the will of man, but of God." John 1:12, 13*

Faith is trusting God, believing His word, appreciating and receiving His love and surrendering fully to Christ thus receiving the free gift of salvation.

> *"For by grace are ye saved through faith; and that not of yourselves: it is the gift of God: Not of works, lest any man should boast. For we are his workmanship, created in Christ Jesus unto good works, which God hath before ordained that we should walk in them." Ephesians 2:8-10.*

> *"That if thou shalt confess with thy mouth the Lord Jesus, and shalt believe in thine heart that God hath raised him from the dead, thou shalt be saved. For with the heart man believeth unto righteousness; and with the mouth confession is made unto salvation. For the scripture saith, Whosoever believeth on him shall not be ashamed. For there is no difference between the Jew and the Greek: for the same Lord over all is*

rich unto all that call upon him. For whosoever shall call upon the name of the Lord shall be saved… So then faith cometh by hearing, and hearing by the word of God." Romans 10: 9-13, 17

The New Birth

The one who truly believes the Gospel cannot continue living for self. There occurs a radical change. The mind (willpower, intellect and emotions) is set free from bondage to self-centredness by the love of God in Christ Jesus. The pull on the mind of the law of sin and death, which is in the flesh, is overcome by the law of the Spirit of life which is in Christ. And whereas before conversion the sin-enslaved mind could not possibly obey God's moral law of love expressed in the Ten Commandments, after conversion the God-centred, love-controlled mind willingly obeys the law of God. In Christ God has rewritten His law of love in the human mind. In Christ the righteousness of the law is fulfilled in the believer.

> *"There is therefore now no condemnation to them which are in Christ Jesus, who walk not after the flesh, but after the Spirit. For the law of the Spirit of life in Christ Jesus hath made me free from the law of sin and death. For what the law could not do, in that it was weak through the flesh, God sending his own Son in the likeness of sinful flesh, and for sin, condemned sin in the flesh: That the righteousness of the law might be fulfilled in us, who walk not after the flesh, but after the Spirit." Romans 8:1-4*

> *"For the love of Christ constraineth us; because we thus judge, that if one died for all, then were all dead:" 2 Cor. 5:14*

> *"I delight to do thy will, O my God: yea, thy law is within my heart." Psalm 40:8*

> *"But his delight is in the law of the Lord; and in his law doth he meditate day and night." Psalm 1:2*

God Has Sought And Found Us In Christ

God made the first move while we were still His enemies. He revealed His absolutely, amazingly, unselfish, unconditional love toward us in sending His Son to redeem us.

"For when we were yet without strength, in due time Christ died for the ungodly. For scarcely for a righteous man will one die: yet peradventure for a good man some would even dare to die. But God commendeth his love toward us, in that, while we were yet sinners, Christ died for us. Much more then, being now justified by his blood, we shall be saved from wrath through him. For if, when we were enemies, we were reconciled to God by the death of his Son, much more, being reconciled, we shall be saved by his life. And not only so, but we also joy in God through our Lord Jesus Christ, by whom we have now received the atonement." Romans 5:6-11

"For all have sinned, and come short of the glory of God;" Romans 3:23

Our salvation does not depend on our initiating or maintaining a relationship with God; it depends on our believing and responding to the relationship He has established with us in Christ!

"Behold, I stand at the door, and knock: if any man hear my voice, and open the door, I will come in to him, and will sup with him, and he with me." Rev. 3:20

Jesus Conquered The Law Of Sin And Death In The Flesh

Jesus came into the world to destroy the works of the devil, and succeeded!

"He that committeth sin is of the devil; for the devil sinneth from the beginning. For this purpose the Son of God was manifested, that he might destroy the works of the devil." 1 John 3:8

"Forasmuch then as the children are partakers of flesh and blood, he also himself likewise took part of the same; that through death he might destroy him that had the power of death, that is, the devil; And deliver them who through fear of death were all their lifetime subject to bondage." Hebrews 2:14, 15.

Our Saviour condemned sin in the flesh thereby conquering the sin problem for the human race. Because of His victory there is now no reason for any human to go on living in sin. The true believer in Christ overcomes all addictions to sin by the love and faith of Jesus!

"What shall we say then? Shall we continue in sin, that grace may abound? God forbid. How shall we, that are dead to sin, live any longer therein?

Know ye not, that so many of us as were baptized into Jesus Christ were baptized into his death? Therefore we are buried with him by baptism into death: that like as Christ was raised up from the dead by the glory of the Father, even so we also should walk in newness of life. For if we have been planted together in the likeness of his death, we shall be also in the likeness of his resurrection: Knowing this, that our old man is crucified with him, that the body of sin might be destroyed, that henceforth we should not serve sin. For he that is dead is freed from sin." Romans 6:1-7.

Faith Works

Faith works. It works by love. We love Him because He first loved us. And since we love Him we trust and surrender fully to let the Holy Spirit cover and fill us with His righteousness.

When temptation comes we therefore reckon ourselves to be dead to sin and we, by the power of His love, expel the tempting thought from our minds before it conceives to produce sin.

Let us now rejoice in these texts of scripture.

"Blessed is the man that endureth temptation: for when he is tried, he shall receive the crown of life, which the Lord hath promised to them that love him. Let no man say when he is tempted, I am tempted of God: for God cannot be tempted with evil, neither tempteth he any man: But every man is tempted, when he is drawn away of his own lust, and enticed. Then when lust hath conceived, it bringeth forth sin: and sin, when it is finished, bringeth forth death." James 1:12-15

"There hath no temptation taken you but such as is common to man: but God is faithful, who will not suffer you to be tempted above that ye are able; but will with the temptation also make a way to escape, that ye may be able to bear it." 1 Cor. 10:13

"For in Jesus Christ neither circumcision availeth any thing, nor uncircumcision; but faith which worketh by love." Gal 5:6

"Likewise reckon ye also yourselves to be dead indeed unto sin, but alive unto God through Jesus Christ our Lord. Let not sin therefore reign in your mortal body, that ye should obey it in the lusts thereof. Neither yield ye your members as instruments of unrighteousness unto sin: but yield yourselves unto God, as those that are alive from the dead, and your

members as instruments of righteousness unto God. For sin shall not have dominion over you: for ye are not under the law, but under grace." Romans 6:11-14

What really is meant by being under grace and not under law?

A person whose relationship with God is under law is a person who seeks to obey the letter of the law by self-effort. The motivation behind such superficial obedience is the motivation of fear of punishment or desire for reward, or both. Such a person obeys because he regards it a duty which must be done in order to be saved. This is legalism.

A person who is under grace is a person who believes with his whole heart, mind, and soul that in Jesus Christ he has full and complete salvation as a free gift. His will is fully surrendered to Christ and his heart is filled with the love of God. Such a person is so thankful to God for the sacrifice of Christ that he cannot contain his love! And motivated by that love he willingly obeys every word of God without fear of punishment or desire for reward. He is so happy and secure in Christ's love that he hates the sins which crucified Christ and lives only to please his Saviour. Grace has transformed him, the old-man of selfishness is crucified and the love of God reigns in his soul, he has the gift of righteousness because he has the indwelling Christ.

> *"Knowing that a man is not justified by the works of the law, but by the faith of Jesus Christ, even we have believed in Jesus Christ, that we might be justified by the faith of Christ, and not by the works of the law: for by the works of the law shall no flesh be justified. But if, while we seek to be justified by Christ, we ourselves also are found sinners, is therefore Christ the minister of sin? God forbid. For if I build again the things which I destroyed, I make myself a transgressor. For I through the law am dead to the law, that I might live unto God. I am crucified with Christ: nevertheless I live; yet not I, but Christ liveth in me: and the life which I now live in the flesh I live by the faith of the Son of God, who loved me, and gave himself for me." Galatians 2:16-20.*

The secret of victory over sin is abiding in Christ. To abide in Christ means to believe in Christ and to surrender one's life, one's heart and will, fully to Christ.

When the believing sinner surrenders to Christ in full faith there occurs a death and a resurrection in his experience. The believer becomes crucified with Christ and dead to the old way of self and sin; and the believer is spiritually resurrected, he receives the Life of Christ through the Holy Spirit. The indwelling Christ lives out His life through the surrendered believer and the righteousness of the law is fulfilled in the believer's life. In other words, receiving the righteousness of Christ by faith is manifested by obedience to all ten commandments!

> *"I am the true vine, and my Father is the husbandman. Every branch in me that beareth not fruit he taketh away: and every branch that beareth fruit, he purgeth it, that it may bring forth more fruit. Now ye are clean through the word which I have spoken unto you. Abide in me, and I in you. As the branch cannot bear fruit of itself, except it abide in the vine; no more can ye, except ye abide in me." John 15:1-4*

> *"If ye love me, keep my commandments." John 14:15*

> *"By this we know that we love the children of God, when we love God, and keep his commandments. For this is the love of God, that we keep his commandments: and his commandments are not grievous. For whatsoever is born of God overcometh the world: and this is the victory that overcometh the world, even our faith." 1 John 5:2-4*

Abiding in Christ means the daily crucifixion of the old man, the self, the ego. By beholding the utterly unselfish, self sacrificing Agapé love revealed at the Cross, the believer is empowered to take up his cross daily, that is, to crucify self, to deny self, to abhor self-love and to be controlled by the selfless Agapé love of Christ and therefore to live the Christ life.

> *"And to all he said, "if anyone wishes to be a follower of mine, he must leave self behind; day after day he must take up his cross, and come with me. Whoever cares for his own safety is lost; but if a man will let himself be lost for my sake, that man is safe." Luke 9:23,24. N.E.B*

The cross means self-denial, death to self, the death of self-love from the soul and its replacement with Divine Love. The soul needs this treatment daily if it is to be transformed by love into a soul which will exhibit righteous behaviour under any circumstance.

God's remedy for sin is rather straightforward.

> *"But God forbid that I should glory, save in the cross of our Lord Jesus Christ, by whom the world is crucified unto me, and I unto the world." Gal. 6:14*

> *"For he that is dead is freed from sin." Rom. 6:7*

The old man, the self, must be crucified.

The old man, the ego, the love of self is continuously seeking to be resurrected and to regain control of the soul under a number of guises. Egocentric religious pride is one of the most deceptive and malignant forms in which the old man may return. This form is the basis of Laodicean lukewarmness.

Since the believer must engage in spiritual warfare against self everyday, Jesus tells us that we must take up our cross daily. This means a daily, in fact, a moment-by-moment surrender of self to the principle of the cross, which is the principle of self-sacrificing love. **This is victory over sin!**

The Good News is that the righteousness of Christ is imputed to us not because of our good works but because of what God has already accomplished for us in Christ. Salvation, righteousness, and eternal life have already been given to all men in Christ. Faith acknowledges God's redemptive work and, in submission, receives the free gift.

The Final Generation Of Living Saints Will Overcome As Christ Overcame

True Christian character perfection, maturity and complete victory over all sin, with the attitude of complete humility and utter dependence on Christ, will characterize the final generation of living saints, called the remnant in Revelation 12:17. They will overcome as He overcame and His character will be fully reproduced in them.

Jesus our risen Saviour is now in the closing stages of His High Priestly ministration in the Heavenly Sanctuary. In order to vindicate God's government He must by virtue of His infinite sacrifice and His High Priestly ministration remove all sin from the experience of His remnant and bring them to perfect maturity of christian character!

> *"To him that overcometh will I grant to sit with me in my throne, even as I also overcame, and am set down with my Father in his throne."*
> *Rev. 3:21*

> *"And he gave some, apostles; and some, prophets; and some, evangelists; and some, pastors and teachers; For the perfecting of the saints, for the work of the ministry, for the edifying of the body of Christ: Till we all come in the unity of the faith, and of the knowledge of the Son of God, unto a perfect man, unto the measure of the stature of the fulness of Christ:" Ephesians 4:11-13*

"Having therefore these promises, dearly beloved, let us cleanse ourselves from all filthiness of the flesh and spirit, perfecting holiness in the fear of God." 2 Corinthians 7:1

"Whosoever committeth sin transgresseth also the law: for sin is the transgression of the law. And ye know that he was manifested to take away our sins; and in him is no sin. Whosoever abideth in him sinneth not: whosoever sinneth hath not seen him, neither known him... Whosoever is born of God doth not commit sin; for his seed remaineth in him: and he cannot sin, because he is born of God. " 1 John 3:4-6, 9

"Be ye therefore perfect, even as your Father which is in heaven is perfect." Matthew 5:48

Twenty

Redemptive Rest and the Character of God

When Adam sinned, corporate humanity in Adam ceased to possess the life of God in the Holy Spirit. The life of God in the Holy Spirit had indwelt Adam's mind, but by choosing Satan's government and rejecting God's government, Adam expelled the life of God from the spirit of his mind. Corporate humanity in Adam became "darkened in their understanding and **alienated** from the **life of God** ..." Eph 4:18.

In addition, physical human life was separated from God's government and would survive temporarily only by virtue of God's mercy exercised through the plan of redemption. In other words physical life became a dying life.

Sin presented a massive problem; it emptied man's mind of the life of God, it separated his physical life from God's government of glory and it stripped him of all righteousness of character.

We have already studied how God has given back His very own righteousness to corporate humanity in Christ. Without any conditions attached God has already redeemed corporate humanity by the faith of Jesus. The individual human being experiences this proffered gift by believing in Jesus! Thus genuine faith works by love to bring the righteousness of Christ into the believer's soul thereby producing love-motivated obedience to all the commandments of God. This love-motivated obedience is the fruit of the gospel and qualifies the believer for fitness for heaven.

Both our title to heaven and our fitness for heaven are found only in the righteousness of God in Christ. God has already entitled and fitted corporate humanity for heaven in Christ. This title and fitness are received by and experienced in the individual believer by the surrender of faith and by the continual abiding in Christ.

"I am the true vine, and my Father is the husbandman. Every branch in me that beareth not fruit he taketh away: and every branch that beareth fruit, he purgeth it, that it may bring forth more fruit. Now ye are clean through the word which I have spoken unto you. Abide in me, and I in you. As the branch cannot bear fruit of itself, except it abide in the vine; no more can ye, except ye abide in me." John 15:1-4

Rest And Redemption

We have already seen that the number seven (7) represents completeness. At the end of creation week the seventh-day Sabbath became the memorial of the eternal principle that all created powers must be **completely** covered and filled with righteousness even as God's eternal power is always covered with His eternal righteousness by His eternal wisdom through His eternal love.

Sin stripped humanity of the righteousness with which man was endowed at creation. In redemption, God has again given His righteousness to corporate humanity in Christ. In Christ corporate humanity is completely covered with God's righteousness. And since seven (7) is God's number of completeness, it means that the seventh-day Sabbath is the memorial of both creation and redemption.

In the beginning of our world the Son of God rested on the seventh-day after six days of creative work.

In the plan of redemption Jesus rested in the tomb on the 7th day after successfully completing the work of redemption as He had rested from labour after successfully completing the work of creation. Then He arose on the first day of the week to begin a new work; the work of His High Priestly ministry for us. (John 14:1-3; Heb. 8:9).

Therefore both in creation and redemption the Son of God rested on the seventh day after the completion of perfect works.

Righteousness is the basis of rest.

"And the work of righteousness shall be peace; and the effect of righteousness quietness and assurance for ever." Isaiah 32:17.

Jesus is our righteousness and Jesus is the Righteousness of God. Jesus is therefore the Source of rest, hence He is Lord of Rest, Lord of the Sabbath.

"But of him are ye in Christ Jesus, who of God is made unto us wisdom, and righteousness, and sanctification, and redemption:" 1 Cor. 1:30

"Come unto me, all ye that labour and are heavy laden, and I will give you rest. Take my yoke upon you, and learn of me; for I am meek and lowly in heart: and ye shall find rest unto your souls." Matt. 11:28, 29

"And he said unto them, The sabbath was made for man, and not man for the sabbath: Therefore the Son of man is Lord also of the sabbath." Mark 2:27, 28

Rest And Justification By Faith

"Now to him that worketh is the reward not reckoned of grace, but of debt. But to him that worketh not, but believeth on him that justifieth the ungodly, his faith is counted for righteousness." Romans 4:4,5

The term "worketh not" is equivalent to "rest." The person who rests his case entirely on the fact that God has accomplished a complete redemption in Christ for all men and who believes on the Lord Jesus Christ, is both counted and made righteous by that faith which rests entirely in Christ.

Thus the Seventh Day Sabbath rest is the sign of justification by faith.

"For we which have believed do enter into rest..."
Hebrews 4: 3 (first Part)

"There remaineth therefore a rest to the people of God. For he that is entered into his rest, he also hath ceased from his own works, as God did from his. Let us labour therefore to enter into that rest, lest any man fall after the same example of unbelief.... For he spake in a certain place of the seventh day on this wise, And God did rest the seventh day from all his works." Hebrews 4:9,10,11, 4

Rest And Sanctification By Faith

The seventh-day Sabbath is always the memorial and sign of God's complete righteousness both in creation and redemption.

"Therefore if any man be in Christ, he is a new creature: old things are passed away; behold, all things are become new." 2 Cor. 5:17

"Moreover, also I gave them my sabbaths, to be a sign between me and them, that they might know that I am the Lord that sanctify them." Ezekiel 20:12

The believer experiences sanctification by appropriating the righteousness of Christ by faith, i.e. by daily, momently yielding his life in living faith to Christ and accepting His power to keep him and His righteousness to fill him.

God wants us to be **completely** covered with His righteousness in Christ so that the shame of our nakedness does not appear.

> "I counsel thee to buy of me gold tried in the fire, that thou mayest be rich; and white raiment, that thou mayest be clothed, and that the shame of thy nakedness do not appear; and anoint thine eyes with eyesalve, that thou mayest see." Rev. 3:18

> "Behold, I come as a thief. Blessed is he that watcheth, and keepeth his garments, lest he walk naked, and they see his shame." Rev. 16:15

Rest And The Government Of God

Rest is the end-result of the righteous use of power, likewise the end product of unrighteousness is **unrest**.

When God's government finishes any work, that work is completely righteous and the result, the effect, is **rest, peace, order and life.**

On the contrary, any work which Satan does is unrighteous and produces unrest, confusion, disorder, destruction and death.

So whereas there is always rest when God finishes a work, there is always unrest and distress when Satan finishes his. The only rest Satan can attempt is a pseudo- or false rest **before** he works because when he finishes work there is unrest and disaster! Satan is the only being in the whole universe who gives his devotees rest before they work.

Therefore, as God's true rest is always celebrated on the seventh-day at the end of the week, Satan's counterfeit or pseudo rest must come on the first day or at the start of the week.

The seventh-day first-day controversy is not merely a matter of which day, but rather a matter of the principles and issues involved in the spiritual warfare between God's government of righteousness and rest and Satan's government of unrighteousness and unrest.

In the end-time the Gospel will produce a remnant who will be sanctified to the level of Christian character maturity and perfection. God's end-time remnant will keep the faith of Jesus and keep the commandments of God and will be completely victorious over all sin. They will also have the patience of Jesus Christ in the face of tremendous odds and threats to their earthly lives. This will be the glorious and fully ripened fruit of the Gospel of which the seventh-day Sabbath is the peculiar sign of the rest found in Christ, the sign of righteousness by faith!

> *"And the dragon was wroth with the woman, and went to make war with the remnant of her seed, which keep the commandments of God, and have the testimony of Jesus Christ." Rev. 12:17*

> *"Here is the patience of the saints: here are they that keep the commandments of God, and the faith of Jesus." Rev. 14:12*

> *"Whosoever abideth in him sinneth not: whosoever sinneth hath not seen him, neither known him." 1 John 3:6*

Satan's end-time followers will reject God's righteousness in Christ and therefore will **not** keep the commandments of God or the faith of Jesus. Church-state legislative enforcement of Sunday-sacredness will be the ultimate manifestation of unrighteousness by works.

> *"And the third angel followed them, saying with a loud voice, If any man worship the beast and his image, and receive his mark in his forehead, or in his hand, The same shall drink of the wine of the wrath of God, which is poured out without mixture into the cup of his indignation; and he shall be tormented with fire and brimstone in the presence of the holy angels, and in the presence of the Lamb: And the smoke of their torment ascendeth up for ever and ever: and they have no rest day nor night, who worship the beast and his image, and whosoever receiveth the mark of his name. Here is the patience of the saints: here are they that keep the commandments of God, and the faith of Jesus." Rev. 14:9-12.*

Absolute Principles

Since *complete* rest is the end-result of righteousness, it is easy to understand why the seventh-day Sabbath must be God's peculiar sign of God's peculiar end-time people called the remnant in Revelation 12:17.

> *"And the dragon was wroth with the woman, and went to make war with the remnant of her seed, which keep the commandments of God, and have the testimony of Jesus Christ." Rev. 12:17*

> *"For we which have believed do enter into rest, as he said, As I have sworn in my wrath, if they shall enter into my rest: although the works were finished from the foundation of the world.*

There remaineth therefore a rest to the people of God. For he that is entered into his rest, he also hath ceased from his own works, as God did from his.

For he spake in a certain place of the seventh day on this wise, And God did rest the seventh day from all his works." Hebrews 4:3,9,10,4

"And the work of righteousness shall be peace; and the effect of righteousness quietness and assurance for ever." Isaiah 32:17

"Great peace have they which love thy law: and nothing shall offend them." Psalm 119:165

And since *total* unrest is the end-result of unrighteousness, the first-day pseudo rest must be the sign of Satan's government of sin and chaos.

"But the wicked are like the troubled sea, when it cannot rest, whose waters cast up mire and dirt. There is no peace, saith my God, to the wicked." Isaiah 57:20,21.

Therefore the final conflict of history will be the controversy over which day is the day of rest and worship for Christians.

The True Sabbath Established By The Faith And Obedience Of Christ

The faith of Jesus and the obedience of Jesus are of the utmost importance to us. The Bible gives us many reasons why the obedience of Christ is so important, let us consider three of them.

1. The obedience of Christ, the righteousness of Christ, justifies the believer in Christ and makes the believer righteous. We are told so in Romans 5:18,19.
    "Therefore as by the offence of one (Adam) judgment came upon all men to condemnation; even so by the righteousness of one (Christ) the free gift came upon all men unto justification of life. For as by one man's disobedience many were made sinners, so BY THE OBEDIENCE OF ONE (CHRIST) SHALL MANY BE MADE RIGHTEOUS." Romans 5:18,19.
2. The obedience of Christ is the PERFECT EXAMPLE which the believer MUST follow if he or she wishes to practice THE TRUE Christianity. We are told so in 1 Peter 2:21.
    "For even here unto were ye called: because Christ also suffered for us, LEAVING US AN EXAMPLE, THAT YE SHOULD FOLLOW HIS STEPS." 1 Peter 2:21.

3. The obedience of Christ is **lived out in the believer's life** by the indwelling Christ through the Holy Spirit. We are told so in Ephesians 3:17 and Galatians 2:20.

    "That Christ may dwell in your hearts by faith; that ye, being rooted and grounded in love, may be able to comprehend with all saints what is the breadth, and length, and depth and height; And to know the love of Christ, which passeth knowledge that ye might be filled with all the fullness of God." Ephesians 3:17-19.

    "I am crucified with Christ: nevertheless I live; yet not I, but Christ liveth in me and the life which I now live in the flesh I live by the faith of the Son of God, who loved me, and gave himself for me." Galatians 2:20.

All this brings us to a very important conclusion, and it is this: **any religious practice, popular though it be, which was not part of the obedience of Christ, cannot be any part of the true Christianity.** Look around at the various denominations of Christianity in the world today and compare their religious practices with the life of Christ and His teachings. You will be surprised at the many popular religious practices which are not part of the obedience of Christ and therefore cannot be any part of the true Christianity.

Consider the matter of baptism. Christ and His disciples practiced baptism by immersion of believers who were old enough to understand, believe, and choose the way of salvation through Christ. Nowhere in the New Testament do we find the slightest hint of baptism of babies by sprinkling or pouring. The practice of infant baptism by sprinkling or pouring or putting a little water on the infant's forehead came from paganism and infiltrated Christianity in the period after the death of the Apostles.

The Apostle Paul had predicted a "falling away" of the early Christian church; read 2 Thessalonians chapter 2. This "falling away" from the purity of New Testament truth occurred gradually at first, and then more rapidly, eventually resulting in the formation of the Roman Christianity that controlled Europe during the Middle Ages.

The churches which teach non-scriptural practices usually claim that they were included into the New Covenant by the **early church fathers**, after the **death** of the Apostles. Such a claim is utterly false.

Jesus Christ established and confirmed the New Covenant or New Testament by His life and death. By His perfect obedience and His sacrificial death He became the author of eternal salvation for the lost race.

The Old Covenant was based upon the **people's promises** to obey by self-effort. The New Covenant was established upon better promises, the promises of God to forgive, cleanse, and make the believing sinner righteous. (Hebrews 8:6-13).

The prophet Daniel had prophesied that Messiah would confirm the covenant for one prophetic week or seven years. (Daniel 9:27).

In establishing the New Covenant, Jesus put into it all that was necessary for the salvation of mankind. During the 3½ years after His death the Apostles accepted, taught and practiced what Christ had given them.

The Apostle Paul explained to the Galatians in Galatians 3:15 that after a covenant has been confirmed nothing can be added to, or, subtracted from it!

Furthermore, Paul told the Hebrews, in Hebrews 9:15-17, that the death of the Testator enforces the Covenant or Testament. And so we understand that the death of Christ confirmed, ratified and enforced the New Covenant, **therefore nothing could be added after his death**! The very first thing Jesus did upon commencing His ministry was to be baptized by immersion in the river Jordan by John the Baptist. He therefore established baptism by immersion as the only true and right type of baptism for the Christian in the New Covenant.

In a similar way we can examine the question of the day of worship for Christians. Sunday keeping was progressively incorporated into Christian practice **long after the death** of Christ and His disciples. Christ kept the seventh-day Sabbath (Luke 4:16, Mark 2:27,28). The disciples, **after the death of Christ,** kept the seventh-day Sabbath, read Luke 23:52 to 56 and Luke 24:1; read also Acts 13:42-44; Acts 16:13; Hebrews 4:4,9,10; Matthew 24:20.

Since it is the **obedience of Christ** which justifies the sinner and establishes the New Covenant; and since Sunday sacredness was NOT part of the obedience of Christ **then sunday keeping cannot be part of the new covenant. And it could not have been rightfully added after christ's death because nothing can be added to the covenant after the death of the testator**!

Sunday keeping is therefore a clever piece of Satanic deception, it is a counterfeit of the real Sabbath. Sunday sacredness is, in fact, pagan in origin and dates back to the days of pagan sun worship. It entered the church during the falling away when Christians compromised with pagans in order to more easily convert them.

Many Christians believe that Sunday is a sign of righteousness by faith. But, in actual fact, it is neither a sign of righteousness nor faith. It was no part of the obedience of Christ and so it is no part of the righteousness of the New Covenant. And second, the evolution of Sunday worship depended upon the works of politicians and Popes. The first Sunday Law was passed politically by the Roman Emperor Constantine in 321 A.D., since then Sunday worship has had to be propped up by religious-political legislation. Sunday worship is most assuredly a sign of unrighteousness by human works based on unbelief of the clear word of God.

The prophet Isaiah prophesied that a time would come when the breach made in God's law would be repaired. And Revelation describes God's final generation of living saints as those who keep the commandments of God and the faith of Jesus. Read Isaiah 58:12-14 and Revelation 14:12.

How Will The Power Of Tradition Be Broken?

Many honest and sincere Christians are so blinded by tradition that it will take something special to open their eyes.

When the Sunday law is passed and when it is enforced by civil penalties, including the death threat, then the light of God's character will penetrate the darkness and the words of Jesus in John 16:1-3 will come ringing down the ages.

> *"These things have I spoken unto you, that ye should not be offended. They shall put you out of the synagogues: yea, the time cometh, that whosoever killeth you will think that he doeth God service. And these things will they do unto you, because they have not known the Father, nor me." John 16:1-3.*

The mere fact that the Sunday Movement will resort to force will mean that it cannot be of God because He does not use force, neither does He threaten to kill those who oppose Him.

What Jesus is saying in John 16:3 is that the true knowledge of God will be critically important in deciding which side of the end-time Sabbath-Sunday controversy is God's side!

Twenty-One

The Wrath of God, Part 2: Absolute Principles

Our God, YAHWEH or JEHOVAH, has made it abundantly clear that He is the One and only true God and His way is the only way of perfect life. The Godhead (The Father, His Son and their Holy Spirit) is infinite in power, wisdom, righteousness, truth and Agapé love.

> *"I am the Lord, and there is none else, there is no God beside me: I girded thee, though thou hast not known me." Isaiah 45:5.*

For any being to be God, that being must be absolutely eternal (beginning-less and endless), self-existent and completely independent of anyone or anything for life. Now remember, YAHWEH God tells us there are no other Gods, He knows of none.

> *"Fear ye not, neither be afraid: have not I told thee from that time, and have declared it? ye are even my witnesses. Is there a God beside me? yea, there is no God; I know not any." Isaiah 44:8.*

Satan claims that creatures can have their own way in opposition to God's way, and NOT die. In fact he claims that such persons will be as gods.

> *"And the serpent said unto the woman, Ye shall not surely die: For God doth know that in the day ye eat thereof, then your eyes shall be opened, and ye shall be as gods, knowing good and evil." Genesis 3:4,5.*

Whoever claims to be a god must (ultimately) be able to maintain himself and his government without outside aid, must be able to have his own way, must be able to maintain his freedom to assert his godhood and to prove his godhood.

Satan contends that each creature can have his own way, the way of self, and it will work. When the creature's self becomes a god, the attitude is to reject the true God. Job 22:15-18 (Notice verse 17).

Sin is putting one's own way before God's way, it is putting self before God. Sin is the transgression of God's law, of God's way, 1 John 3:4; Isaiah 53:6; 2 Cor. 5:15.

God has a very simple foolproof way of dealing with those who claim to be gods, those who want their own way. Yes, He has a very simple way of testing any so-called better way than His way. All He has to do is to leave the person alone to his/her own way, and if they continue to exist on their own, then that person would have to be a **real** god with a **right** way, but if the person and the person's way collapse to destruction it would prove after all, that the person was only a creature who needed God and God's way for survival.

Since finite creatures are absolutely dependent on the Infinite Creator for existence, then the Infinite Creator would have to do everything necessary to maintain the life and well-being of finite creatures. If the Infinite Creator leaves His creatures **alone** they **will** perish; they **must** perish.

To think that God must use some other method than withdrawal to get rid of sin is to insult His power, wisdom and love; it is because He is infinite and creatures are finite that His creatures need Him and cannot survive without Him.

So when people say that God must do something, other than withdraw, to get rid of Satan, sinners and sin, they are insulting God and showing their ignorance of the issues in the Great Conflict between right and wrong.

If God has to do anything at all to destroy the sinner other than leave the sinner alone then His power is less than infinite, He is less than God. The proof that **He** is God, and **no one else**, is that just by His doing nothing everything else would perish!

> *"And, Thou, Lord, in the beginning hast laid the foundation of the earth; and the heavens are the works of thine hands: They shall perish; but thou remainest; and they all shall wax old as doth a garment; And as a vesture shalt thou fold them up, and they shall be changed: but thou art the same, and thy years shall not fail." Hebrews 1:10-12*

> *"Of old hast thou laid the foundation of the earth: and the heavens are the work of thy hands. They shall perish, but thou shalt endure: yea, all of them shall wax old like a garment; as a vesture shalt thou change them,*

and they shall be changed: But thou art the same, and thy years shall have no end." Psalm 102:25-27.

The proof of the Infinite God is that He has to do everything to keep finite creatures alive. If God should do nothing, i.e. withdraw his maintaining, upholding power, creatures will perish, Col. 1:17. Since all things hold together in Him when He lets go things fall apart. (Psalm 121)

To suggest that sinful creatures can survive when fully and ultimately separated from God or that God has to do something else to destroy the sinner other than complete separation is to suggest that creatures can survive without God and that sin is harmless. This is a heresy as old as the Devil! On the contrary, God says:

> *"But he that sinneth against me wrongeth his own soul: all they that hate me love death." Proverbs 8:36*

> *"O Lord, the hope of Israel, all that forsake thee shall be ashamed, and they that depart from me shall be written in the earth, because they have forsaken the Lord, the fountain of living waters." Jeremiah 17:13*

> *"O Israel, thou hast destroyed thyself; but in me is thine help." Hosea 13:9*

Since God is without beginning or end, then His way must be the only absolute way of life; the only absolutely right way. When creatures reject God's way they are rejecting God's righteousness and therefore rejecting life. God has made us free to choose and He will respect our choice. Ultimately those who reject God will be left alone to the gods of their choosing—"ownwayness" is death!

> *"For they that are after the flesh do mind the things of the flesh; but they that are after the Spirit the things of the Spirit. For to be carnally minded is death; but to be spiritually minded is life and peace." Rom. 8:5,6*

> *"He that believeth on the Son hath everlasting life: and he that believeth not the Son shall not see life; but the wrath of God abideth on him." John 3:36*

To reject God's righteousness in any area or detail of our lives is to tell God that we can handle that area of our lives without Him. It is to tell Him to leave us alone in that area. It is to tell Him that we are gods in that area of our lives. (James 2:8-12). Full surrender to God's will is eternal life. (John 5:30). To sow the wind will be to reap the whirlwind. Hosea 8:7.

In mercy God pleads with us to change our minds, to accept all of His righteousness in Christ. Since God's righteousness is a whole unit, to reject any small part is to eventually reject all. James 2:10. If we persist in having our own way God will eventually have to say "Ephraim is joined to idols: **leave him alone**." Hosea 4:17.

Any sin which we do not overcome will eventually overcome us and work our own ruin by separating us from God.

> *"Be not deceived; God is not mocked: for whatsoever a man soweth, that shall he also reap. For he that soweth to his flesh shall of the flesh reap corruption; but he that soweth to the Spirit shall of the Spirit reap life everlasting. And let us not be weary in well doing: for in due season we shall reap, if we faint not." Galatians 6:7-9.*

When men choose their own way, they place themselves in controversy with God. They will have no place in the kingdom of heaven, for they are at war with the very principles of heaven. In disregarding the will of God, they are placing themselves on the side of Satan, the enemy of God and man. Not by one word, not by many words, but by every word that God has spoken, shall man live. We cannot disregard one word, however trifling it may seem to us, and be safe. There is not a commandment of the law that is not for the good and happiness of man, both in this life and in the life to come. In obedience to God's law, man is surrounded as with a hedge and kept from the evil. He who breaks down this divinely erected barrier at any point has destroyed its power to protect him for he has opened a way by which the enemy can enter to waste and ruin.

And remember, only in Christ is the righteousness of the law fulfilled in the believer's character through faith which works by love.

> *"For in Jesus Christ neither circumcision availeth any thing, nor uncircumcision; but faith which worketh by love." Galatians 5:6*

> *"That the righteousness of the law might be fulfilled in us, who walk not after the flesh, but after the Spirit." Romans 8:4*

> *"For this is the love of God, that we keep his commandments: and his commandments are not grievous." 1 John 5:3*

The Basis And Threefold Function Of Grace Or Mercy

Because of what God has accomplished for, and given to, humanity in Christ, there is an atmosphere of grace or mercy surrounding our world as real as the atmosphere of air which we breathe! This atmosphere of grace is the omnipresence and work of the Holy Spirit and it also includes the holy angels of God through whom the Holy Spirit works. The Holy Spirit also works through those human beings who abide in Christ. This atmosphere of grace is therefore one vast protective hedge of angels with the Holy Spirit working in and through each angel to perform a threefold function.

First, the Holy Spirit sustains life on this sinful planet.

Second, the Holy Spirit channels blessings through the angels to our world while at the same time He restrains the forces of evil, including human passion and the sin-spoiled forces of nature.

Third, the Holy Spirit, through angels and through the church, invites, draws, and woos all men to receive Christ as their personal Saviour and Lord.

These three functions though distinct are intricately inter-related and are fundamentally inseparable. We should at this stage review the Biblical proof for everything we have said so far.

> "It is of the Lord's mercies that we are not consumed, because his compassions fail not. They are new every morning: great is thy faithfulness. The Lord is my portion, saith my soul; therefore will I hope in him." Lam. 3:22-24

> "The angel of the Lord encampeth round about them that fear him, and delivereth them." Psalm 34:7

> "Are they not all ministering spirits, sent forth to minister for them who shall be heirs of salvation?" Hebrews 1:14

> "Nevertheless I tell you the truth; It is expedient for you that I go away: for if I go not away, the Comforter will not come unto you; but if I depart, I will send him unto you. And when he is come, he will reprove the world of sin, and of righteousness, and of judgment:

> Howbeit when he, the Spirit of truth, is come, he will guide you into all truth: for he shall not speak of himself; but whatsoever he shall hear, that shall he speak: and he will shew you things to come. He shall glorify me: for he shall receive of mine, and shall shew it unto you." John 16:7,8,13,14

"And the Spirit and the bride say, Come. And let him that heareth say, Come. And let him that is athirst come. And whosoever will, let him take the water of life freely." Rev. 22:17

"Likewise the Spirit also helpeth our infirmities: for we know not what we should pray for as we ought: but the Spirit itself maketh intercession for us with groanings which cannot be uttered. And he that searcheth the hearts knoweth what is the mind of the Spirit, because he maketh intercession for the saints according to the will of God." Romans 8:26-27.

The Three Final Stages Of Separation Or Wrath

Separation from God's mercy occurs in the reverse order of the functions of mercy or grace.

First, there is separation from the drawing, convicting, inviting and pleading work of the Holy Spirit upon the human spirit, soul, mind and heart. So the Spirit's third function is the first to be cut off by persistent sin. Second there is sin's separation from the Spirit's protecting, restraining work and third, there is separation from the Spirit's life sustaining function which is His first work. Let us examine these three stages of wrath in some detail.

Stage One Of Final Wrath

The persistent indulgence in sin, unbelief of truth, or belief in error is at first met with increasing appeals and a deeper conviction of truth and righteousness by the Holy Spirit. But if these appeals are resisted there is a gradual and progressive hardening of the sinner's heart against the Spirit's work of drawing the soul to Christ and His truth and righteousness. And the heart is left to the consequences of its hardness. Eventually the sinner's thinking process or thought pattern becomes fixed in error and sin and therefore becomes separated from the Spirit's work of truth and righteousness. This is the sin against the Holy Spirit also called the unpardonable sin.

"And grieve not the Holy Spirit of God, whereby ye are sealed unto the day of redemption." Eph. 4:30

"Wherefore I say unto you, All manner of sin and blasphemy shall be forgiven unto men: but the blasphemy against the Holy Ghost shall not be forgiven unto men. And whosoever speaketh a word against the Son of man, it shall be forgiven him: but whosoever speaketh against the Holy Ghost, it shall not be forgiven him, neither in this world, neither in the world to come." Matthew 12:31,32

"For it is impossible for those who were once enlightened, and have tasted of the heavenly gift, and were made partakers of the Holy Ghost, And have tasted the good word of God, and the powers of the world to come, If they shall fall away, to renew them again unto repentance; seeing they crucify to themselves the Son of God afresh, and put him to an open shame." Heb. 6:4-6

"And the Lord said, My spirit shall not always strive with man." Genesis 6;3 (first part)

This sin was committed by individuals, families and nations in the past. Some outstanding examples mentioned in scripture would be: Cain, King Saul, Baalam, Ananias and Sapphira, Sodom and Gomorrah, Jerusalem in A.D. 70; and the antediluvian world.

Of course, this sin against, and separation from, the Spirit's convicting and convincing work will climax at the close of general human probation after the great final warning goes forth to all the world.

"He that is unjust, let him be unjust still: and he which is filthy, let him be filthy still: and he that is righteous, let him be righteous still: and he that is holy, let him be holy still. And, behold, I come quickly; and my reward is with me, to give every man according as his work shall be." Rev. 22:11,12

Stage Two Of Final Wrath

This stage of separation or wrath follows stage one. In this stage there is sin's separation from the Spirit's protecting and restraining work. The Spirit's work of blessing and protecting humans and restraining the forces of evil is withdrawn. This produces physical destruction and death (the first death).

The antediluvian world suffered this second stage of wrath after the first stage, similar to Sodom and Gomorrah and Jerusalem in A.D.70. This stage was also the basis of the fall of nations, which had previously risen to supremacy.

In the end-time this stage will occur after the close of probation and will result in the loosening of the global angelic hedge thereby allowing the forces of evil to collapse progressively in the development or "pouring out" of the seven last plagues.

"And after these things I saw four angels standing on the four corners of the earth, holding the four winds of the earth, that the wind should not blow on the earth, nor on the sea, nor on any tree. And I saw another angel ascending from the east, having the seal of the living God: and he cried with a loud voice to the four angels, to whom it was given to hurt the earth and the sea, Saying, Hurt not the earth, neither the sea, nor the trees, till we have sealed the servants of our God in their foreheads." Rev. 7:1-3

"And I saw another sign in heaven, great and marvellous, seven angels having the seven last plagues; for in them is filled up the wrath of God." Rev. 15:1

Stage Three Of Final Wrath

This final stage of wrath will occur at the end of the 1000 years of Revelation 20 when there will be complete withdrawal of, or separation from, the Spirit's life-sustaining function. This will result in the second death.

In this third stage of wrath the previous two stages are included, i.e. there is ultimate and total separation from God by sin.

Whereas in the past individuals and nations have suffered the first two stages of wrath and are awaiting stage three, which will occur after the second resurrection, only one man, the Man Christ Jesus, has suffered the full and complete separation from God by our sins.

No one needs to die the second death, because Jesus has already suffered that death for all men. But those who reject Christ will suffer that death and sadly they will be the majority.

"For God so loved the world, that he gave his only begotten Son, that whosoever believeth in him should not perish, but have everlasting life." John 3:16

"He that believeth on the Son hath everlasting life: and he that believeth not the Son shall not see life; but the wrath of God abideth on him." John 3:36

Other Considerations

In order to show His ancient people the terrible and inevitable results of sin, many a time God withdrew partially and allowed their enemies to defeat them or some other calamity to befall them to arouse them to repentance. Yet they continued downhill until their final national destruction in A.D. 70.

In the case of Job, God handed Job over to the enemy to prove his loyalty and therefore to defeat Satan in his false charges against God.

Absolute Freedom

God made His intelligent creatures free moral agents to choose His way or their own way. God is truly a God of absolute freedom and He has given His intelligent creatures genuine, absolute freedom of choice.

Genuine freedom of choice means that there are at least two options. Each option must carry its intrinsic consequences. God's way is the only way of life because it is the only right way. Life, not death, is in the way of righteousness.

> "In the way of righteousness is life; and in the pathway thereof there is no death." Proverbs 12:28

Satan's way of selfishness is the way which opposes and separates from the way of life. It is the way of death.

> "Then when lust hath conceived, it bringeth forth sin: and sin, when it is finished, bringeth forth death." James 1:15

> "For the wages of sin is death; but the gift of God is eternal life through Jesus Christ our Lord." Romans 6:23

> "Be not deceived; God is not mocked: for whatsoever a man soweth, that shall he also reap. For he that soweth to his flesh shall of the flesh reap corruption; but he that soweth to the Spirit shall of the Spirit reap life everlasting." Galatians 6:7,8

God could not claim to have made us free if He kills us for exercising our freedom of choice. Such a claim would be a farce.

But He has made us free. Free to accept His life in Christ or free to reject it. And if a man rejects life can he survive? Would anyone have to kill him?

> "And this is the record, that God hath given to us eternal life, and this life is in his Son. He that hath the Son hath life; and he that hath not the Son of God hath not life." 1 John 5:11,12

> "Blessed and holy is he that hath part in the first resurrection: on such the second death hath no power, but they shall be priests of God and of Christ, and shall reign with him a thousand years." Rev. 20:6

Twenty-two

In Christ God Has Given Us His Own Life

When the Son of God took on our human flesh he took on our body and brain with the natural biochemical and biophysical mechanism of the thinking process. And yet, through the natural human mind-structure (brain chemistry), He produced sinless, divine or spiritual mind-function (motives, thoughts, character)!

In producing perfect sinless character, Jesus had to continuously and constantly overcome the law of sin and death in the flesh of both His body and brain. Paul makes this clear in Romans 8:3, when he says that Jesus condemned sin in the flesh.

Since Jesus had a human brain and mind-structure, He therefore had the mind-structure of a human self-will always struggling for expression through His mind-function. But He surrendered constantly to His Father in full faith and thereby performed not His human will but the will of His Father. (John 5:30; 6:38; Matthew 26:39). In other words, He allowed the mind-function of God to be manifested through the mind-structure of human nature. And this was the essence of the "mind of Christ."

The Bible speaks of the "spirit of the mind" (Ephesians 4:23). All ordinary descendants of Adam have been conceived and born with a spiritually dead human spirit (Eph 2:1-5; 4:18) and therefore all stand in need of conversion, of the renewing of the spirit of the mind (Eph. 4:23).

But the man Christ Jesus was not born spiritually dead in the spirit of His mind. In the incarnation, the Word or Wisdom of YAHWEH became flesh. At the conception of Jesus in the Virgin's womb, the Divine Nature, Life and Personality of the Second Person of the Godhead became mysteriously (and incomprehensibly) blended with the human spirit of the human being. Paul makes this clear in 1 Cor. 15:45-47 where he says that the first man Adam was made a living soul; the last Adam was made a quickening spirit. The first man was of the earth, earthly: the second is the Lord from heaven!

Because the Second Person of the Godhead was fused to the spirit of the man Christ Jesus, He received the Holy Spirit without measure and the Father indwelt in Him by the Holy Spirit. (John 3:34: 14:10).

Throughout His earthly life He constantly and continuously submitted the human mind-structure to the will of the Father through the Holy Spirit. In other words every tempting thought suggested by the law of sin and death in body and brain was repulsed and expelled with the thoughts of God. Herein were the sufferings by which Jesus learned obedience. He submitted the human mind (soul) to the will of God and in Him we have this victorious sanctification of the mind (soul).

In Gethsemane, the human self-will exerted its last desperate struggle to control His mind-function but with an incomprehensible agony Jesus again submitted Himself fully to the will of His Father. And by the time He died on Calvary He had fully united the Divine mind with the human mind – the redemption of the human soul was accomplished.

When he died on the cross, the human life was given up to the second death (Romans 6:23). In the resurrection the life of His Spirit, which was the life of God, became the life of the new body—the redemption of the human body was accomplished! (Romans 8:10,11).

What a glorious redemption of spirit, soul and body!

Christ, the Son of God, became the Son of man; He who was one with the Father became One with us; He who was Spirit was manifested in the flesh: He who was the likeness of God was made in the likeness of men; the Righteousness of God was made to be sin; The Source of all blessing was made a curse: higher than all the universe, yet made lower than the angels; The One in whom is all wisdom, knowledge and understanding was made to learn obedience; The King of glory taking the place of a Servant to sinful man. The Source of all life was made a dependent receiver. All this for man! Oh what Love! Behold such amazing love! Such love is beyond the realm of man: This is the unique, self-sacrificing, Agapé Love of God! Praise the LORD!

In His incarnation, The Son of God condescended to the lowest level in order to reconcile man to God. Man was at the lowest level and unless Christ had gone there He could not have reached those He came to save. It would have been an almost infinite sacrifice if Christ had come as man before Adam had fallen. Yet Christ went beyond and partook of humanity, not only after the fall but when the human race had experienced four thousand years of degeneration. Still this was not all. Christ exercised His love toward us in that He went to our death, even the death of the cross. At the cross there was such a sundering of the Divine Powers that all heaven quaked. However, in death, Christ won the victory: Christ vanquished the power of the enemy. The Father's government stands secure, His character vindicated and salvation for the human race assured.

Christ was nailed to the cross, but He gained the victory. The whole force of evil gathered itself together in an effort to destroy Him who was the Light of the world, the Truth that makes men wise unto salvation. But no advantage was gained by this confederacy. With every advance move, Satan was bringing nearer his eternal ruin. Christ was indeed enduring the contradiction of sinners against Himself. But every pang of suffering that He bore helped tear away the foundation of the enemy's kingdom. Satan bruised Christ's heel, but Christ bruised Satan's head. Through death the Saviour destroyed him that had the power of death. In the very act of grasping its prey, death was vanquished; for by dying, Christ brought life and immortality to light thus establishing the gospel.

An Infinite Sacrifice

Jesus Christ made an infinite sacrifice for our redemption. Jesus took two natures and two lives to the cross: the Divine Nature and Life, and the human nature and physical human life.

At the cross the human nature with its physical life died whereas the Divine Nature with its Eternal Life did not die. Yet all of Christ remained in the grave. The Divine Nature and Life could not have functioned as a person because His humanity had died. There was therefore an interruption in the communication between the Father and Son producing infinite pain to the Father's heart of love.

The life that died was the physical human life. The life that He laid down was His Divine Eternal Life. (John 10:15; 1 John 3:16).

And the life by which He came forth from the grave was the Divine Eternal Life (John 10:17,18). This means that the new body possessed the very life of God as verily as the old body possessed the human physical life. Therefore, in the same way as the physical human nature and life formed the natural infrastructure of the old body, so the Divine Nature and Life formed the spiritual infrastructure of the resurrected new body of our Lord.

O what infinite love!

Sin had written off human life.

And wonder of wonders! God has given to us His own life in Jesus Christ. In the resurrection – translation event at the Second Coming of Christ, the redeemed will receive new, real, spiritual, glorified bodies, eternally alive, incorruptible and immortal with the very life of God!

> *"And this is the record, that God hath given to us eternal life, and this life is in his Son. He that hath the Son hath life; and he that hath not the Son of God hath not life." 1 John 5:11, 12*

> *"For our conversation is in heaven; from whence also we look for the Saviour, the Lord Jesus Christ: Who shall change our vile body, that it may be fashioned like unto his glorious body, according to the working whereby he is able even to subdue all things unto himself." Philippians 3:20, 21*

> *"So also is the resurrection of the dead. It is sown in corruption; it is raised in incorruption: It is sown in dishonour; it is raised in glory: it is sown in weakness; it is raised in power: It is sown a natural body; it is raised a spiritual body. There is a natural body, and there is a spiritual body.*

> *"And so it is written, The first man Adam was made a living soul; the last Adam was made a quickening spirit. Howbeit that was not first which is spiritual, but that which is natural; and afterward that which is spiritual. The first man is of the earth, earthy: the second man is the Lord from heaven.*

> *"As is the earthy, such are they also that are earthy: and as is the heavenly, such are they also that are heavenly. And as we have borne the image of the earthy, we shall also bear the image of the heavenly.*

> *"For this corruptible must put on incorruption, and this mortal must put on immortality. So when this corruptible shall have put on incorruption, and this mortal shall have put on immortality, then shall be brought to pass the saying that is written, Death is swallowed up in victory." 1 Cor. 15:42-49, 53,54.*

What an infinite gift! What infinite Love! God's eternal self-sacrificing love has given His own life in His Son to us. Such knowledge gives the believer the motive power to endure all the attacks of the enemy for the Lord's sake.

> *"For which cause we faint not; but though our outward man perish, yet the inward man is renewed day by day. For our light affliction, which is but for a moment, worketh for us a far more exceeding and eternal weight of glory.*

"While we look not at the things which are seen, but at the things which are not seen: for the things which are seen are temporal; but the things which are not seen are eternal." 2 Cor. 4:16, 17, 18.

God's Eternal Purpose — A Synopsis

From all eternity past God foresaw the development of the sin problem and from all eternity past He had devised the plan of redemption. God's eternal purpose is all-embracing and has been so from all eternity past. It included creation and redemption as well as all the glorious accomplishments of redemption.

From all eternity past, God foreknew the choices of each and all of His creatures and therefore His eternal purpose included the progressive revelation of His love in order to effectively deal with the choices of His creatures.

"And to make all men see what is the fellowship of the mystery, which from the beginning of the world hath been hid in God, who created all things by Jesus Christ: To the intent that now unto the principalities and powers in heavenly places might be known by the church the manifold wisdom of God, According to the eternal purpose which he purposed in Christ Jesus our Lord:" Eph. 3:9-11.

"Having made known unto us the mystery of his will, according to his good pleasure which he hath purposed in himself: That in the dispensation of the fulness of times he might gather together in one all things in Christ, both which are in heaven, and which are on earth; even in him: In whom also we have obtained an inheritance, being predestinated according to the purpose of him who worketh all things after the counsel of his own will: That we should be to the praise of his glory, who first trusted in Christ." Eph. 1:9-12.

"Even the mystery which hath been hid from ages and from generations, but now is made manifest to his saints: To whom God would make known what is the riches of the glory of this mystery among the Gentiles; which is Christ in you, the hope of glory:" Col. 1:26,27.

God can successfully solve any problem and overcome any opposition to His government. And he does so only in righteousness and love without interfering with the freedom of choice of his intelligent creatures, and without force (Zech 4:6).

God's eternal purpose is conceived in infinite Wisdom, is filled with infinite Righteousness and Truth; is motivated by infinite love and is backed up by infinite power used harmlessly and righteously without by-passing the principles of freedom of choice.

Such a plan cannot fail – 1 Cor. 13:8; 2 Cor. 13:8; Rom. 8:31,28; Rom. 4:20,21; Eph. 1:11.

And yet God leaves His creatures absolutely free to choose for or against His eternal purpose.

THOSE WHO REJECT HIM AND HIS PLAN WRITE THEMSELVES OFF. Jeremiah 17:13.

FOR THOSE WHO SURRENDER TO HIM AND HIS PLAN ALL THINGS WORK TOGETHER FOR GOOD!

"And we know that all things work together for good to them that love God, to them who are the called according to his purpose." Romans 8:28

One of the most glorious mysteries about God is that opposition enhances the ultimate victory of His plan, even though the process of overcoming the opposition must necessarily include self-sacrificial suffering. John 12:24.

In the great controversy, God employs His eternal self-sacrificing love to solve problems by His eternal wisdom. He does not use violent compulsory force. He employs His power righteously, by His love, without invading even to a hair's breadth, His creatures' freedom. (To selfish man this method seems foolish and weak; 1 Cor. 1:25-28).

The greater the opposition and the evil, the more love and wisdom God applies to the problem. When God applies greater love and wisdom, the result is that **more** is achieved than if the problem had never occurred! Therefore 2 Cor. 13:8 is an absolute principle of the Divine Nature.

Examples of this glorious truth are found in Gen. 45:5-8; 50:20; and also Ruth.

Similarly, the challenge of the sin problem has been turned by God into an overwhelming victory for His government; redemptive exaltation of the redeemed; and eternal security of the Universe in the eternity to come.

The redemptive results of God's eternal purpose will be an eternal testimony to God's mercy, eternal proof of His infinite wisdom and the eternal manifestation of His infinitely self-sacrificing love and suffering for the good of His creatures.

Indeed sin can never again arise in the universe (Nahum 1:9). Love's self sacrifice has produced eternal immunity against sin ever developing in the eternity to come.

Moreover, God will have a generic family all of His own because redeemed humanity will possess the life of God in mind and body and will share His throne!

Indeed the redeemed will be more closely connected to God than if sin had never occurred! Hallelujah!

> *"Who shall separate us from the love of Christ? Shall tribulation, or distress, or persecution, or famine, or nakedness, or peril, or sword?*
>
> *As it is written, For thy sake we are killed all the day long; we are accounted as sheep for the slaughter.*
>
> *Nay, in all these things we are more than conquerors through him that loved us.*
>
> *For I am persuaded, that neither death, nor life, nor angels, nor principalities, nor powers, nor things present, nor things to come,*
>
> *Nor height, nor depth, nor any other creature, shall be able to separate us from the love of God, which is in Christ Jesus our Lord."*
> *Romans 8:35-39*

Twenty-three

God's Character and the Mystery of Suffering

The eternal principle which is the foundation of God's throne is the principle of self-sacrificing love. This is the law of life for God and the universe. God is love and love is life.

In the Great Controversy God rests His case on Love's application of Wisdom, Righteousness and Truth to power. He will use His power only righteously, which is harmlessly (Romans 13:8,10). And He allows His creatures full freedom; freedom to think, to choose, to decide.

For those who choose God's way of using power wisely and righteously by love, He gives them His Love and Righteousness as free gifts *in Christ through the Holy Spirit.*

For those who reject his way, He leaves them free to follow their own way but He "bends over backward" to convince them of His way. If they ultimately reject Him, He will ultimately and absolutely leave them alone, and that will be the second death.

Because Love gives all of itself and because Love rests its case on **right** rather than **might,** Love is open to hurt and to the sacrifice of itself. **This the principle of the cross.**

Even in the beginning, when there was no sin, the God of love first ran the risk by making all His creatures free. He foresaw that sin would develop and would cost Him infinite suffering, but there was no other way for love to travel than the path of self-sacrifice, the path of the cross.

To sinful, selfish creatures (on planet Earth), love's self-sacrifice seems like defeat and looks like foolishness. But in love's self-sacrifice are the seeds of eternal life.

Selfishness is always trying to save self. But in the self-saving of selfishness there are the seeds of eternal death. Luke 9:23,24.

The Satanic government of self-centredness attacks God's government of selfless love with falsehood and deception, and ultimately, with brute force and violence. But love defends not itself, it simply rests its case upon wisdom, righteousness and truth.

Divine Power always rests in Wisdom through Love, and Power's rest in Wisdom, is always victorious through Love by the pathway of self-sacrifice.

Because God is love then love must be eternal and never-failing, 1 John 4:8,16; 1 Corinthians 13:8. And since love rests its case upon truth and right then love can never be defeated 2 Corinthians 13:8.

We live in a moral universe, one in which the law of Love is supreme and in which the law of love fulfils every obligation to each being in the universe, whether to God or His creatures.

As we have already learned, Agapé love, the Divine eternal love of God, is the love which loves because of its own inherent nature and not because of the excellence or worth of its object. This love is not primarily an emotion but is active, benevolent, sacrificial, out-going goodwill, working by the application of wisdom, righteousness and truth to power. The love of God is spontaneous, automatic love. God loves us unconditionally not because of who we are but because of who He is. It is His nature to love. Matthew 5:45.

There is no love without self-giving. There is no self-giving without the risk of being hurt. In our free and moral universe, in which the great conflict is in progress there can be no love without suffering. Suffering is an essential ingredient of love's victorious conflict with selfishness. God has not loved without cost. The Father and the Son suffered infinite pain in the sacrifice made to save mankind and to ensure a sinless universe in the eternity to come! 2 Corinthians 5:21; Romans 8:32; 1 Corinthians 13:4.

The Importance Of Suffering

The Church is being prepared to sit with Christ on His throne. In order to qualify for this exalted position of co-rulership with Christ in the future eternity, the church, the Bride of Christ, must be conformed to His image. Rev. 3:21; Rom. 8:29,30; Eph. 5:27.

The members of the church must be conformed to the image of the Son first in character, while probation lasts, and second in body at the Second Coming of Christ. If the members of the church, the body of Christ, are to qualify for their future ministry to the universe in the eternity to come, then they must share the character of God Himself which is the character of Agapé love. And as we have already learned, the character of Agapé love cannot be developed in fallen humanity without suffering.

Christ Himself won the victory through the pathway of suffering. Heb. 2:10; 5:8. Union with Christ in His sufferings is the pre-requisite to union with Christ in His glory, in other words, the cross is the means by which glory is achieved! 2 Tim. 2:12; Romans 5:1-5.

In the human experience there can be no character development without suffering, therefore suffering is absolutely necessary for the future enthronement of the church.

Why The Need For Suffering

When God made Adam, He pronounced him very good. God's unselfish love, in the Holy Spirit, filled and controlled Adam's spirit and soul. But the fall produced massive damage to Adam and all humanity. By accepting Satan's lies, Adam and all mankind became SELF-CENTRED.

Self-centredness is the very essence of all sin and it results in self-destruction. Isaiah 14:12-15; James 1:15.

Sin originated in self-exaltation. Ezekiel 28:17.

Selfishness is death. Romans 8:6 (first part).

Self-centredness is the central foundation of hostility which is the basis of hell. Self-centredness issues forth into pride, hatred, violence, the exaltation of self by deception and by force, and ultimately, self-centredness, self-destructs (the second death). Romans 8:5-7; James 1:15.

In conforming an individual to the image of His Son, God must cleanse him of self-centredness. This begins at initial justification and the new birth, and continues in the process of sanctification. Philippians 1:6; 1 Thess. 5:23.

How Suffering And Tribulation Work To Decentralize Us

Sufferings and tribulation, failure and disappointment, sickness and death, all show us that we are nothing; that we cannot save ourselves; that we need to surrender to Someone greater than we are. Suffering therefore breaks down self-centred pride and works on the personality in such a way as to change it from being ego-centric to being Deo-centric. But all this depends upon the attitude of the person.

Sufferings and tribulation, especially annoyances, frustrations, delays, and disappointments also work upon us to expose deep-seated, self-centred defects such as: impatience, intolerance, cruelty, roughness, impoliteness, retaliation, self-protectiveness, greed, anger, and the desire for self-exaltation. These defects must be acknowledged, repented of, confessed, and cleansed out of the soul.

By recognizing our nothingness and our ugliness of character, we will have a deeper sense of our need of Christ and His righteous character of love and humility.

Moreover, the believer must keep his mind fixed on Christ and His life-giving character of love. If the eye of faith is kept fixed on Christ and if the believer practices the attributes of divine love under every difficulty then there occurs the progressive growth in Agapé love that prepares the soul for glory.

Another important work of suffering and tribulation is that since they show us our nothingness, we will better appreciate the privilege of prayer. Prayer may be considered as an attitude of total dependence upon God which issues forth in communication with God. In every problem we are to see a call to prayer, that is, we are to recognize our helplessness and seek the all-sufficiency of God.

Through adversity, prayer and study of God's word we will develop a close, intimate union with Christ. And the Holy Spirit will impart the love and righteousness and humility of Christ into our souls.

One's Reaction To Adversity Determines The Results

Many people waste the wonderful opportunities for character building which adversity offers. Rather than allowing the Holy Spirit to use the adversity to change them from self-centredness to God-centredness, they entrench themselves in self-pity and ego-centric, attention-seeking techniques. They therefore become self-defensive, sensitive and devoid of any rest of soul.

On the other hand, suffering, from whatever source, whatever nature, and whatever intensity, plus submissive acceptance and surrender to God, produces Christlike character!

Affliction, triumphantly accepted in the present time, produces the qualifications needed for the extremely high rank which the redeemed will enjoy in the eternity to come. This is true because God uses adversity to slay and cast out the self-life, so that the believer is delivered from self-centredness and pride and is set free to love.

In the light of all which we have been learning in these lectures, it should be clear that murmuring, complaining, fretfulness, and discontent are all self-destructive and sinful.

The Apostle Paul advised his Corinthian congregation:

"Neither murmur ye, as some of them also murmured, and were destroyed of the destroyer." 1 Cor. 10:10.

Since *"our light affliction…. Worketh for us a far more exceeding and eternal weight of glory"* (2 Cor. 4:17) and since we eagerly look forward to the glory to come, we should allow affliction to work for us by cheerfully submitting to God for His refining work on our souls.

An Ever-Deepening Death To Self

Union with Christ on the cross means suffering with Him and for Him. Union with Christ on the cross means an ever-deepening death to self and sin. The more empty we are, the more we can be filled with the fullness of God's self-sacrificing love and humility. The Apostle Paul gives a clear analysis of these principles in Romans 6 and Galatians 5:16-19.

The faith which remains surrendered to the principle of self-sacrificing love under all circumstances, even under abuse, persecution, torture and in the face of death, is called in the Bible *"Gold tried with fire."* 1 Peter 1:7.

Such faith works by love to purify the soul (Gal. 5:6) and brings to the believer the victory of Christ which overcomes the world (1 John 5:4,5). This is the faith which thanks God and praises Him, even in adversity, thereby releasing the power of the gospel which is the power of God unto salvation from sin to those who believe (Romans 1:16,17). This is the faith of Jesus (Rev. 14:12), the gold which He freely gives to us to cure us of our lukewarmness (Rev. 3:18). He says to us, *"I counsel thee to buy of me gold tried in the fire."* Rev, 3:18.

This faith of Jesus was made perfect through His (Jesus) sufferings (Hebrews 2:10). In other words, in Christ the gold has been tried in the fire and brought to its greatest possible purity. Such faith therefore enables the believer to be "tried in the fire" and emerge victorious (Rev. 3:12).

In the Christian warfare the battle to be won is the battle against self. At initial conversion, self is dethroned and love enthroned in the spirit of the human soul. But deep in the conscious and unconscious minds are defects of character; the hereditary and acquired tendencies to serve self, defend self, assert self, depend on self, retaliate for the protection of human ego. All these defects must be cleansed out of our minds and be replaced with the beautiful attributes of divine love mentioned in 1 Cor. 13. **Only when the soul is thus cleansed of all the deep-seated defects of character, will the lovely character of christ be fully reflected in and through the human soul.**

The believer's victory is the victory of Christ. It is to be received as a free gift. It is not obtained by self-effort or by works. The victory is obtained by faith through prayer and study of God's word and through the various trials and temptations and crises of life. The troubles and calamities of life are caused by sin but are permitted by God and used by Him to show us the deep-seated defects in our souls that we may repent, confess, and, by faith, receive deeper infillings of the righteousness of Christ. This refining work is being supervised by our High Priest in the Most Holy Place of the Heavenly Sanctuary, where since 1844 He has been patiently performing the work of preparing His final generation of living saints.

Laodicean lukewarmness has delayed this work for over a century, but Christ will at last achieve what the Prophet Malachi foretold in Malachi 3:3,4.

As we learn, believe and receive the truth, our souls and spirits are cleansed of sin and filled with truth and righteousness until the character of Christ is fully reproduced in us. When this happens then the Heavenly sanctuary will be cleansed of our sin and the seal of God fixed in our foreheads; that means that by our choice the Holy Spirit will have fixed, with permanence, the righteousness of Christ within the human spirit and mind. To this end, Jesus, our High Priest in the Most Holy Place, performs the work of "a refiner and purifier of silver." There are certain attributes of character which cannot be fully developed in redeemed human beings without trials, adversity and fierce temptations. The Christian may read about patience, longsuffering, endurance, and perseverance in the Bible and think he is alright in these areas just by studying the word. But Christ, our High Priest, will permit trials, adversity and temptations to come upon the believer to show him the deep-seated defects of character in the soul and provide him with the very experiences needed for the development of genuine divine patience, meekness, and humility. The great men and women of God in the Bible all underwent this refining process by which they were brought to higher experiences in character perfection and closer intimacy with God through Christ by the Holy Spirit. **Christ himself, the captain of our salvation, was perfected in faith through sufferings and this faith he offers to us as a free gift. It is gold that has been purified in fire. And for us to fully reflect this faith of Jesus we need suffering too.** 1 Peter 1:3-12; Hebrews 2:10.

This brings us to a very important point. **Since the believer is surrendered completely to God, the Christian must thank God for, and praise Him in adversity.** Rather than impulsively ask for deliverance from the adversity, the Christian ought to thank God and praise him for the refining work being done on him for the purpose of perfecting character. This is the mind of submissive faith, the faith of Christ, that must be exercised in adversity in order for patience to be fully developed to the Christ-like standard. James 1:1-4; Rom. 8:31-39.

So we see then that it is through believing and receiving the word of God, through trials and adversity, that the soul is cleansed of every defect of character and filled with the truth until the character of Christ is fully reproduced in and reflected through the sanctified soul.

The Patience of the Saints in the Final Crisis

God overcomes evil with good. Our Lord Jesus Christ endured all the suffering, pain and death which Satan's government could have inflicted upon Him in His death on the cross. That was the decisive battle and the decisive victory. The battle was fought and the victory won. Satan used force, cruelty and deception; Christ overcame by employing love, truth and righteousness.

The Church, the Body of Christ, must also endure its share of suffering in the process of defeating Satan's government without force.

> *"Who now rejoice in my sufferings for you, and fill up that which is behind of the afflictions of Christ in my flesh for his body's sake, which is the church." Col. 1:24.*

Satan's human agencies will carry themselves beyond the boundary of God's life-sustaining, protective mercy by their onslaught of cruelty, violence and force upon the remnant people of God in the end time.

God's final generation of living saints will understand this and will therefore exercise patience during the final crisis.

Knowing that God will not intervene arbitrarily, that He will not put down rebellion by force but that He allows those who do not want Him to depart from Him thereby cutting themselves off from His life-sustaining grace, the saints will understand that they must wait patiently for sin to run its course of separation from God until all earthly governments collapse to utter ruin.

> *"And the seventh angel sounded; and there were great voices in heaven, saying, The kingdoms of this world are become the kingdoms of our Lord, and of his Christ; and he shall reign for ever and ever." Rev. 11:15.*

Twenty-four

The Final Battle In The Great Controversy

The Decisive Battle

Christ's victory on the cross decided the outcome of the Great Controversy between God's government and Satan's. Christ's victory was both decisive and incisive. Satan's government was defeated and utterly so. And he was defeated not by the power of might but by the power of right. In killing the Son of God, Satan's government wrote itself off! In dying, Christ triumphed over the forces of iniquity!

> *"Forasmuch then as the children are partakers of flesh and blood, he also himself likewise took part of the same; that through death he might destroy him that had the power of death, that is, the devil; And deliver them who through fear of death were all their lifetime subject to bondage." Hebrews 2:14,15.*

> *"And having spoiled principalities and powers, he made a shew of them openly, triumphing over them in it." Colossians 2:15*

> *"He that committeth sin is of the devil; for the devil sinneth from the beginning. For this purpose the Son of God was manifested, that he might destroy the works of the devil." 1 John 3:8*

Satan's charges against God's government were all shown to be false. The Man Christ Jesus, by His sinless life in our sinful flesh and by His infinite sacrifice on the cross, proved that God would go to whatever depth was required to save man. In giving His Son, God gave all. Moreover, God in the Person of His Son suffered the infinite pain of the death which sin causes in order to save the lost race from destruction.

"Behold, what manner of love the Father hath bestowed upon us, that we should be called the sons of God: therefore the world knoweth us not, because it knew him not." 1 John 3:1.

Such love is without a parallel. Children of the heavenly King! The matchless love of God for a world that did not love Him. This is a theme for the most profound meditation! It has a subduing power upon the soul and brings the mind into captivity to the will of God. The more we study the character of God in the light of the cross, the more we see mercy, tenderness, and forgiveness blended with equity and justice and the more clearly we discern innumerable evidences of a love that is infinite and a tender pity that infinitely surpasses a mother's yearning sympathy for her wayward child.

The Conclusive Battle

Can the Gospel of Jesus Christ reproduce His victory in His Body, the church? Can the decisive victory won by Christ produce a final generation of believers who will overcome as He overcame by making His victory their own by faith? Will there be a final generation of living saints whose character will be the character of Agapé self-sacrificing love as Christ's was?

Scripture answers YES!

"Forasmuch then as Christ hath suffered for us in the flesh, arm yourselves likewise with the same mind: for he that hath suffered in the flesh hath ceased from sin; That he no longer should live the rest of his time in the flesh to the lusts of men, but to the will of God." 1 Peter 4:1,2

"To him that overcometh will I grant to sit with me in my throne, even as I also overcame, and am set down with my Father in his throne." Rev. 3:21.

There will be a conclusive battle. The final generation of true believers called the remnant of the woman's seed in Revelation 12:17 will be the subject of ultimate Satanic aggressive warfare. Satan will make war with the remnant because they will keep the commandments of God and the faith or testimony of Jesus.

"And the dragon was wroth with the woman, and went to make war with the remnant of her seed, which keep the commandments of God, and have the testimony of Jesus Christ." Rev. 12:17.

God Is Now Waiting For And Preparing This Remnant

The Bible describes three special final messages which must prepare God's final or remnant people. These messages are written down in Revelation 14: 6-12, the messages of three angels.

The foundation of this threefold warning is the everlasting gospel of God's love revealed in what He has done for, and given to, mankind in Christ.

> *"And I saw another angel fly in the midst of heaven, having the everlasting gospel to preach unto them that dwell on the earth, and to every nation, and kindred, and tongue, and people," Rev. 14:6.*

This first angel's message announces the judgement and invites all men to worship God as Creator and Saviour in Jesus Christ.

> *"Saying with a loud voice, Fear God, and give glory to him; for the hour of his judgment is come: and worship him that made heaven, and earth, and the sea, and the fountains of waters." Rev. 14:7.*

The second angel's message announces Babylon's fall. Babylon is false religion including false Christianity and it must fall because error and sin are self-destructive.

> *"And there followed another angel, saying, Babylon is fallen, is fallen, that great city, because she made all nations drink of the wine of the wrath of her fornication." Rev. 14:8.*

The third angel warns against the image and mark of the best.

> *"And the third angel followed them, saying with a loud voice, If any man worship the beast and his image, and receive his mark in his forehead, or in his hand, The same shall drink of the wine of the wrath of God, which is poured out without mixture into the cup of his indignation; and he shall be tormented with fire and brimstone in the presence of the holy angels, and in the presence of the Lamb: And the smoke of their torment ascendeth up for ever and ever: and they have no rest day nor night, who worship the beast and his image, and whosoever receiveth the mark of his name." Rev. 14:9,10,11.*

The mark of the beast system will obviously transgress the commandments of God because, in contrast to those who receive the mark of the beast, the saints are described as patiently keeping the commandments of God.

"Here is the patience of the saints: here are they that keep the commandments of God, and the faith of Jesus." Rev. 14:12.

Moreover, the worshippers of the beast will be devoid of rest, therefore the mark of the beast must be the end-time enforcement of transgression of God's Seventh-Day Sabbath which is the sign of rest in the righteousness of Christ.

God Is Waiting For A Sealed People

The vast majority of people in this world are fully committed to Satan's government. According to the principles of absolute freedom, God must ultimately give up this world to its chosen government of sin.

But He is waiting. He is waiting for His end-time servants to be sealed in the foreheads with the seal of the living God!

"And after these things I saw four angels standing on the four corners of the earth, holding the four winds of the earth, that the wind should not blow on the earth, nor on the sea, nor on any tree. And I saw another angel ascending from the east, having the seal of the living God: and he cried with a loud voice to the four angels, to whom it was given to hurt the earth and the sea, Saying, Hurt not the earth, neither the sea, nor the trees, till we have sealed the servants of our God in their foreheads." Rev. 7:1-3.

This sealed group called the 144,000 will have Christ's Father's name written in their foreheads. They will have the true knowledge of God's character both intellectually and experientially and will completely reflect the victorious righteousness of Christ.

"And I looked, and, lo, a Lamb stood on the mount Sion, and with him an hundred forty and four thousand, having his Father's name written in their foreheads." Rev. 14:1.

The truth of righteousness by faith will produce a Christian character maturity and perfection in the true end-time remnant!

Worldwide Religious Agitation

The enforcement of Sunday laws will evoke a vigorous response from God's people. Those most advanced in the truth will, under the latter-rain of the Holy Spirit, give the great final warning thereby calling all of God's true honest people to separate from all error and sin and to fully receive the righteousness of Christ which will be manifested in obedience to all Ten Commandments.

> *"And after these things I saw another angel come down from heaven, having great power; and the earth was lightened with his glory. And he cried mightily with a strong voice, saying, Babylon the great is fallen, is fallen, and is become the habitation of devils, and the hold of every foul spirit, and a cage of every unclean and hateful bird. For all nations have drunk of the wine of the wrath of her fornication, and the kings of the earth have committed fornication with her, and the merchants of the earth are waxed rich through the abundance of her delicacies. And I heard another voice from heaven, saying, Come out of her, my people, that ye be not partakers of her sins, and that ye receive not of her plagues." Rev. 18:1-4.*

Victory Over Lukewarmness

God's people must by then have obtained the full victory over Laodicean pride and lukewarmness. They must fully receive the faith and love of Christ, the righteousness of Christ and the spiritual discernment of Christ.

> *"I counsel thee to buy of me gold tried in the fire, that thou mayest be rich; and white raiment, that thou mayest be clothed, and that the shame of thy nakedness do not appear; and anoint thine eyes with eyesalve, that thou mayest see. As many as I love, I rebuke and chasten: be zealous therefore, and repent... To him that overcometh will I grant to sit with me in my throne, even as I also overcame, and am set down with my Father in his throne." Rev. 3:18,19,21.*

The message of God's character revealed in the victorious righteousness of Christ in the everlasting Gospel guarantees deliverance from lukewarmness to those who genuinely believe!

> *"Having therefore these promises, dearly beloved, let us cleanse ourselves from all filthiness of the flesh and spirit, perfecting holiness in the fear of God." 2 Cor. 7:1*

> *"Repent ye therefore, and be converted, that your sins may be blotted out, when the times of refreshing shall come from the presence of the Lord; And he shall send Jesus Christ, which before was preached unto you:" Acts 3:19,20.*

The eradication of all deep-seated sinful defects of character and the infilling with the righteousness of Christ are the two dimensions of the sealing work .

The Cleansing Of The Heavenly Sanctuary

In an ancient prophecy written down in Daniel 8:13,14 it was prophesied that the "sanctuary would be cleansed" or would "emerge victorious" after 2300 years. The 2300 years started in 457B.C and ended in 1844 October. We are therefore living in the **time** of the "cleansing of the sanctuary."

In the earthly Old Testament sanctuary the priests performed a daily ministry. In addition there was a once yearly ministry performed by the High Priest alone who went into the Most Holy Place of the sanctuary on the Day of Atonement to cleanse away all the sins that had "accumulated" in the sanctuary by confessions throughout the year.

Paul explains in Hebrews Chapter 9 that those Old Testament services were a figure or model of the New Testament Melchisedek ministry of Jesus in the Heavenly sanctuary.

> *"Now of the things which we have spoken this is the sum: We have such an high priest, who is set on the right hand of the throne of the Majesty in the heavens;" Hebrews 8:1.*

From the time of His ascension to the end of the 2300 years Christ performed His continuous intercessory ministry in the first apartment of the Heavenly sanctuary. But since 1844 Christ has been officiating in the second apartment of the Heavenly Sanctuary.

The Vindication Of God's Government

The Heavenly Sanctuary is the Headquarters of God's government and the Control Centre for the universe. God's government and His sanctuary have been blamed by Satan for sin and its consequences.

Christ's decisive victory would have cleared the sanctuary of all Satan's charges. But one question remains. Satan argues that what God has accomplished in Christ cannot be reproduced in His church.

In order to vindicate His government; in order to cleanse the sanctuary of any blame for sin, God must produce a victorious remnant fully reflecting the love and righteousness of Christ.

We can be sure of one thing; the remnant will be united in their understanding of the true character of God as revealed in Christ. They will know that God is not to be blamed for, and is not the cause of sin or death. They will fully reflect God's agapé love and righteousness to the world thereby proving Satan wrong and God right, bringing the world to the final point of decision. All confessed sins and all blame for sin and evil will be "cleansed" out of the sanctuary and put on Satan and his government.

The Close Of Probation

When every mind has been made up for or against God's righteousness, probation will close.

The four angels will loose the four winds of the earth - the forces of evil - and unimaginable and progressive destruction, called the seven last plagues, will develop.

The mark-of-the-beast system will sentence God's people to death but they will be delivered by God's voice and Christ will return in blazing glory to take His resurrected and translated saints to heaven for the 1000 years of Revelation 20.

At the end of the millennial reign in Heaven, Christ, and the Holy City with God the Father and all the Holy Angels will come down to earth. The unsaved will be resurrected to hear their final judgement before the great white throne.

Then God will totally give up all the unsaved, the separation will be complete, and in the final fires of destruction caused by that separation; the unsaved will die the second death.

Sin and sinners will be no more. Love's self-sacrifice would have conquered all!

And Can It Be

And can it be that I should gain
An interest in the Saviour's blood?
Died He for me, who caused His pain?
For me, who Him to death persued?
Amazing love! How can it be
That Thou, my God shouldst die for me?

Refrain
Amazing love! How can it be
That Thou, my God, shouldst die for me

He left His Father's throne above,
So free, so infinite His grace;
Emptied Himself of all but love,
And bled for Adam's helpless race;
Tis mercy all, immense and free;
For, O my God, it found out me.

Long my imprisioned spirit lay
Fast bound in sin and nature's night;
Thine eye diffused a quick'ning ray,
I woke the dungeon flamed with light;
My chains fell off, my heart was free;
I rose, went forth and followed Thee.

No condemnation now I dread;
Jesus and all in Him, is mine!
Alive in Him, my living Head,
And clothed in righteousness divine,
Bold I approach the eternal throne,
And claim the crown, through Christ my own.

By Charles Wesley

Publications Available from
Truth For the Final Generation

The Powerful Message of the Two Covenants in the Doctrine of Righteousness by Faith

This book seeks to show the difference between the Old and New Covenants, but more importantly to show how loving, compassionate, merciful, and sweet is our gracious God who is not only able but eager to fulfill His promises in our lives.

The Sealing Work in the Final Generation

The sealing work begins at conversion when the believer's name is entered into the Book of Life. For the final generation, the sealing ends with the believer's name being retained in the Book of Life, after he has passed the great final test and has demonstrated that his mind is fully fixed in loyalty to God.

Elect According to the Foreknowledge of God

Election, predestination and free choice are subjects that have agitated the minds of God's people down through the centuries of the Christian era. If God has foreknown all things are we really free to choose? Is there a true doctrine of predestination? Christians want to make their calling and election sure. Who are the elect? This book seeks to give the Biblical answers to these questions.

The Power of God's Word in the Science of Faith

Many Christians drift along in a superficial experience without appreciating the power of God's word. In this series of studies we discover the victorious power in God's word, and learn to receive and employ that power in the work of overcoming sin.

The New World Economic Order—How Will it Affect You?

The coming new world economic order will usher in sweeping changes to our accustomed way of life, especially the liberties we have enjoyed over the past two hundred years. Necessary reading for the new century.

The Proclamation of the Acceptable Year of the Lord

Discussions include studies of the Harvest principle and the Generation concept. They examine the reasons for the long delay of the Second Advent and what must be our responsibilities if we are to hasten the day of the Lord and finish the work early in this new generation.

Other books and publications are available: contact us for details